IF YOU
Leave THIS
Farm

IF YOU
Leave THIS
Farm

THE DREAM IS DESTROYED

Amanda Farmer

ARCHWAY
PUBLISHING

Archway Publishing books may be ordered through booksellers or by contacting:

Archway Publishing
1663 Liberty Drive
Bloomington, IN 47403
www.archwaypublishing.com
1-(888)-242-5904

ISBN: 978-1-4808-0929-1 (e)
ISBN: 978-1-4808-0928-4 (sc)
ISBN: 978-1-4808-0930-7 (hc)

Library of Congress Control Number: 2014912946

Printed in the United States of America

Archway Publishing rev. date: 7/23/2014

Contents

Preface

This is my true story of being raised in the Mennonite faith by a patriarchal father. I did not realize as a child that there was anything different about our family from other Mennonites, and I embraced the beliefs and expectations that had been integrated into my life. My journey has its beginnings in Pennsylvania, where I was born, but it really doesn't begin until we move to Minnesota to farm together. This is the story of our move to Minnesota, the conflicts that developed there, and my struggle to leave the farm. It is also a story about the challenges and triumphs of farming.

Leaving the farm, though, resulted in consequences I did not foresee and would never have predicted in a Christian family. The sequel to this book will continue the story of the disintegration of the family as a result of unresolved expectations resulting from my and my brother's leaving the farm. This is one story of what can happen when one child stays on the farm, and the others leave to begin a different life.

The names in this book have been changed to protect the dignity and privacy of those involved. The area for the setting in Minnesota has also been changed or made ambiguous for the same reason. This book and its sequel are not, under any circumstances, meant to be used as a reprisal or an opportunity to be vindictive. Rather, they exist to share a story with others, a story that, I hope, can provide insight and understanding into the difficulties that can arise in families who attempt to mingle their personal lives and their futures together. My hope is that my story will prevent other families from going down this path—to hurt and bitterness and estrangement.

Chapter 1

THE EARLY YEARS

*I*t is April 1973, and it is dark outside as I slide my feet out of bed at four o'clock in the morning and dress hurriedly in the brightly lit bathroom. Daddy is already out at the barn and expecting his children to show up to help with milking, feeding the growing cattle, and giving milk replacer to the younger calves. I awaken Joseph, my brother who is fourteen and just a year younger than I, by banging on the bathroom wall that adjoins his bedroom. I hear a stirring, so I make my way downstairs and prepare for my mad dash through the dark to the barn to avoid the monsters that might be waiting for me. Paul, at seventeen and two years older than I, is allowed to continue sleeping and will appear later.

Our farm of one hundred twenty-five acres is located in the rolling hills of southern Pennsylvania. A narrow blacktop road twists through the farmstead, its path wandering within twenty feet of the buildings. The white clapboard house sits several hundred feet down the road from the typical red-bank barn. The upper part of the barn houses tons of hay and straw placed there through hours of toiling together during the hot summer months. The lower part is the milking area, which contains twenty-eight stanchions for holding the cows securely in place while they are milked. We are modern farmers in that the milk goes directly from the milking machine into a glass pipeline above the stanchions. The milk shoots through the glass tube to the holding jar in the milk house, is pumped through a filter, and then is dumped directly into the bulk milk tank. We milk around one hundred twenty-five cows twice each day. When the cows are not being milked, they are housed in a large free-stall barn. They are fed silage twice a day using a squirming auger that crawls down the middle of the feed bunk. The silage cascades down a chute from the two towering concrete silos that grace the landscape.

With the milking chores done, I make a repeat dash back to the house at around six forty-five. Mama works nights as a nurse at the hospital and will not arrive home until after eight thirty, leaving no one to greet me at the door. The house seems cold and forbidding in these dark, silent early hours of morning. My first action is to throw on several lights. Nobody seems to be lurking in any of the rooms, so I make an effort to slow down my frantic breathing. The bus is due at seven fifteen. I must hurry to wash up and change clothes.

Paul and Joseph are soon back in the house as well, and Paul makes a kettle of instant oatmeal for our breakfast. Oatmeal almost makes me gag, but there is no time to find something else to eat. I take a small portion and slather it with brown sugar, hoping to slide it past my palate as quickly as possible. There is always shoofly pie, made by Mama each week for breakfast dessert, and that is what I go for as sustenance for the day. Joseph and I check frequently out the western house window for the flashing red lights of the school bus at the neighbor's as we gulp our food. Lunch boxes and coats lie by the door. I just finish shoving my second arm into a coat sleeve as the bus screeches to a halt outside our door. My stomach is curled in knots from this frantic rush each morning. But now it is time for my nap. We are the second ones on the school bus. I settle into a seat with Joseph for our thirty-five minute ride to Friendship High School, located in rural south-central Pennsylvania. This long ride gives me the perfect opportunity to make up a few of those missed winks of sleep. It has been impressed on us that work is more important than sleep. And it is certainly much more important than school. Therefore, this year—my tenth—will be my last year in school. Paul was removed from school on a work permit three years earlier and Joseph and I will leave next year to stay home and help on the farm too. I am being allowed to stay in school a year longer than the boys because I am smart—or maybe because I am a girl. I am not really sure which. Mama has a bachelor's degree in nursing, but Daddy does not believe that education is important. After all, he only has an eighth-grade education, and he did "just fine." And apparently, Mama doesn't think it necessary or prudent to oppose his wishes.

In some ways, I hate school. The lack of sleep and the stress of not having time to properly do the schoolwork weigh on me. But school does provide a means for me to explore a world that is quite different from my home life. There are the usual classes offered at any public high school: English, German, typing, geometry, social studies, gym class, and study hall. I learn easily and don't need to put a lot of brain power into mastering the material. This ability saves me scholastically, since I am always exhausted from the early-morning hours spent in the barn. My eyelids flutter as each successive teacher drones on; my head nods and finally sinks onto my desk. If there were a category in the *Guinness Book of World Records* for number of classes slept through, I would receive it. Surprisingly, I receive little reprimand from my teachers, probably because I ace most of their tests and make straight As except in gym class.

Oh yes, gym class is my bane. But how can I make an A in gym when I am the only one wearing a dress while trying to climb a rope or perform cartwheels? We are Mennonites, so every day, I wear a skirt and blouse as my basic attire. A single braid of uncut hair snakes down my back beyond my waist. It is capped by a small mesh "covering" on my head.

Mennonites are distinguishable from other Christian denominations primarily by several beliefs that are distinct. They were, historically, called Anabaptists because of their rejection of infant baptism and the practice of believer's baptism. The Mennonite Christian is to be separate from the world in all practices. This translates into a strict belief in the separation of church and state and the practice of non-resistance. No church member may serve in the military, participate in a lawsuit, vote, or hold public office. Dressing differently from the world is also stressed. For women, this means they are not to "use makeup, cut their hair, and wear slacks, shorts, or fashionable head dress, short sleeves, low necklines, dresses not reaching well below the knees, or clothes that expose the form of the body in an immodest way. The hair is to be covered with a veil of sufficient size to adequately cover the head." (Excerpted from the Statement of Christian Doctrine and Rules and Discipline, Lancaster Conference of the Mennonite Church, July 17, 1968.)

In spite of feeling like a misfit at school, I do have a small, select group of "worldly" friends. Cory, Laura, and I hang out together in study hall, and they are my confidants. However, I am not allowed to visit their homes or go places with them because they might influence me toward those worldly ways. But a sense of personal pride does come with the stellar grades I am able to make in my classes, and it gains me a certain respect with my peers. My accomplishment, though, is barely given a nod at home when I present my report card for signing.

After school, Joseph and I have a thirty-minute wait while our bus makes its first run before returning to pick us up for our ride home. I pull out the homework assigned for today and work on it while waiting. I finish it on the bus ride home, as I know there will not be time for homework once we arrive home. It is about four o'clock in the afternoon when the bus drops Joseph and me off at our house. We are expected to change clothes and go to the barn immediately to do chores again.

Afternoon is Mama's sleeping time, so she is curled up in bed. I tiptoe into the bedroom and nudge Mama to ask if I can have a cookie—or whatever else my eyes spy in the kitchen that looks good for a snack. She always just mumbles, "yes" and goes back to sleep. As we eat our snack, Joseph and I turn on the radio to a Christian station out of southeastern Pennsylvania. It is time for *Ranger Bill*. I love *Ranger Bill*. It is filled with adventure, something that I long for. We listen with absorption while we keep an eye on the road, hoping to hear the final minutes of resolution before Daddy appears, wondering why we are not out to the barn yet.

Today, though, we make it through the end of the radio program without Daddy appearing, and I jump on my bicycle for a quick ride to the barn. It is my speedy, dependable means of transportation around the farm. The sun is warm, and daffodils are just starting to emerge by the well house. The smell of freshly moved dirt is in the air. Daddy and Paul are out in the field working ground and getting ready to plant corn.

That means I will have to milk alone tonight while Joseph feeds the young stock. Milking goes so much more slowly when there is no one to help. I am relieved when Daddy comes into the barn around eight o'clock and helps to wrap up the chores.

Daddy is a man who commands respect. He expects his

children to obey him, and nonsense is not tolerated. Daddy could best be described as frugal and hardworking. His five-foot, nine-inch stature is trim and lined with bulging muscles. For as long as I can remember, Daddy has been totally bald. Only a strip of black hair caresses his ears and circles around the back of his head—a head that is too small for even the smallest "one size fits all" seed-corn cap. But having a small head has not in any way diminished his keen business sense.

Soon Paul, Joseph, and I are racing each other to the house on our bicycles for supper. Mama has supper on the stove and is napping while she waits for us. She will feed us and clean up before heading off to work again for another night shift. Mama is physically short and plump. Her dark-brown hair is pulled back under the traditional Mennonite veiling. Her round, smiling face greets us each day while her hands perform the never-ending tasks of cooking and cleaning and washing, as well as working away from home. I never hear Mama complain about her daily routine.

I grab a book to read while supper is being put on the table. Reading is my escape to adventures I probably will never see, but there is nothing to stop me from dreaming. I work in a few paragraphs before it is time to gather at the table. Daddy begins by reading a passage aloud from the Bible. Then he prays before we dig into a hearty meal of farmer's fare: potatoes, meat, a vegetable, and always a dessert.

"Children," Daddy says tonight, "Next Monday evening, we are going to go to Nirvana to see some slides of farms that are for sale in the Midwest. They are being shown by a real estate agent from there. I need you to get the milking started right away when you get home from school."

Daddy has been talking for some time now about buying land "out West" and moving out of the crowded Pennsylvania area. Currently, Daddy is renting land in small blocks of five to ten acres, as far away as twenty miles from the home farm. He and Paul are farming around five hundred acres altogether. We all spend a lot of time on the road, traveling back and forth to the various fields and hauling the baled hay home during the long summer days. Daddy and Paul think it would be so much easier to just have a piece of land all in one block to farm. I am not so sure about this idea, but Daddy promises that if we do this, we won't milk as many cows. We will only have maybe fifty cows. That sounds like a wonderful idea to me and I am open to an adventure. By now it is nine thirty, and I fall into bed, exhausted with dreams of faraway places and fewer cows to milk.

The spring of 1973 has flowed into summer, slipped through fall, and another winter is knocking on our doorstep. I watch for the postman with eagerness and rush out of the house as soon as I see him pull away from the mailbox. Yesterday, Paul, Joseph, and I did not get a letter; but today, it is waiting. I rip it open and read:

Dear Children,   *November 12, 1973, 9:15 a.m.*

Greetings in Jesus's Precious Name,
We got to Garvin at 12:00 noon. Ate dinner with them then went to church ninety miles away. There were about five different families attending. One came over from … Wisconsin, 120 miles away. Peter Wiehler. They are moving into this area. Eight children, oldest twenty-one. Benjamin Penner has five children. Two are married and aren't out here. They have an eighteen-year-old boy. A fifteen-year-old girl, Ellen Sue, and two blind

boys ... I think they are eleven and twelve years old ...
We slept at this home. We used our electric blanket again.
They live in a rented house. The one on their farm needs a
lot of work to be done.

We just saw a 1200 acre farm. Four-bedroom house.
The family has nine children, so the place looks dirty and
a mess. I hope we don't have to get rid of all the trash
around. Only one bathroom. Outbuildings aren't bad. It's
a grain, beef, and hog farm. $650 an acre. We want to go
back to this farm tomorrow to talk to the owner. Roads
all around it. Joseph and Amanda could drive and drive
without fear of hitting anything or turning over ...

With love, Daddy and Mama

I fold the letter and begin making dinner for my brothers. Daddy and Mama have been gone since November 9. This is their second trip out West this year; this time targeting Minnesota with the objective of buying a farm there. We have been left at home again to milk and care for the house and farm while they are gone. I feel grown-up and respected to be entrusted with so much responsibility by our parents. From my perspective as a young teenager, I see our family as a tight-knit, generally happy family. Our life revolves mostly around working together. And working hard and willingly is the ticket to Daddy's approval. Though we have little playtime, no vacations, and little contact with the outside world, it has never occurred to me that this is not a normal state of affairs. In fact, in the autobiography that I wrote for an English assignment in my last year in the public school, I concluded with "there is no generation gap in our family."

We had waved good-bye to Mama and Daddy for their first fact-finding farm search on August 17. We were left alone for the first time in our lives to do the milking and farm work and to keep the home fires burning. Their trip involved making a large loop through the Midwest, looking at farms in every state from Ohio, Indiana, Illinois, and Wisconsin to Minnesota and back through Iowa, Oklahoma, and Tennessee. In each state, they made note of the crops and the various farms on the market. It had been an awesome year for crops in Minnesota. They reported that Minnesota had the best crops of anywhere that they traveled. So Daddy and Mama came home on August 26 having made the decision to make Minnesota our new farming home.

The intent of this return trip in November is to find the perfect farm to buy. Our Pennsylvania farm has been on the market since September 29, and Daddy is hoping for a fast and profitable sale. He is asking $270,000 for the one hundred twenty-five acres. That would make a good down payment on whatever farm they purchase. I can tell by the letter in my hand that Daddy and Mama see this land that she writes about as becoming ours. And sure enough, when they return on November 16, they report that they have bought the 1,280-acre farm in Minnesota. I am excited by the progress. This seems like a great adventure to me, and with anticipation, I look forward to beginning this new journey.

Chapter 2

THE MOVING ADVENTURE

*I*t is January 27, 1974. Today, as soon as the morning milking is done, I head out to resume clipping the cows' hair, in preparation for the sale of the milk cows coming up in a week. The plan is to sell the adult milking cows but transport the thirty pregnant heifers and other young cattle to Minnesota. It is too hard to truck animals that are lactating over twelve hundred miles. The trip takes at least twenty-two hours, and trying to stop and unload to milk would be a huge hassle. Besides, there are no milking facilities on the farm that Daddy bought. Those will need to be built the first summer.

The dairy cows must look neat and clean so that the buyers will want to pay the highest prices for them. This is the fourth straight day for me of meticulously clipping the hair off of the heads and udders of each cow. I am becoming truly weary of this. Some of them stand quietly, but then there are those that dance this way and that. I get slammed between cows, kicked occasionally, and bumped around with their hard heads. I have bruises everywhere and cramps in my back and legs. Joseph, my lean, brown-tousled-hair brother, has been commissioned to help me, but he has no interest in this work and doesn't really care if every hair is removed. So there have been harsh words from Daddy and sullen foot dragging from Joseph, making the job even more stressful. But I have a sense of satisfaction tonight as I finish the last cow. I have clipped around one hundred cows, and they look sleek as they line up in their stalls for milking.

We have wasted no time in preparing for our move after Daddy and Mama's return from Minnesota. The months of December and January are filled with planning for the sale—testing cows for tuberculosis and pregnancy, vaccinating calves, updating Dairy Herd Improvement Association (DHIA) records, and getting the registration papers in order for those cows that are registered with the American Holstein association. Books and jars and clothes and every other thing a farm family can possibly accumulate over the course of twelve years must be packed in between all the activities of getting the herd ready for disposal.

In the few spare moments remaining, I work on the high school correspondence course that I started in September from a school out of Chicago, Illinois. This course will supply me with a piece of paper that says I have completed high school. I am told, though, that if I ever want to go to nursing school, the diploma from this school will probably not be accepted as a valid graduation certificate for entrance. But I have no intention of becoming a nurse. I am happy with being a farmer, so I brush off the comment with little additional thought. I find the material easy and speed through the lessons.

Paul, at eighteen, is tall and thin. His blue eyes are always moving along with his body—a constant flurry of activity. Paul is struggling to finish his courses, which he started over three years ago. He can't seem to find the desire to sit still long enough to tackle his last required subject, bookkeeping. Mama is encouraging all of us to get our schooling done before we move, but

Paul has no time for books anymore. I realize I have a knack for numbers and love manipulating them, so I decide to help him out with his remaining course. I wonder if the school thinks it funny that his grades really improve with his last subject. Anyway, I am relieved that studying is over when my diploma arrives in the mail on January 15. I can now put my full attention toward helping with the move.

The cold takes my breath away as I step out on the porch in the darkness before dawn. I peek at the thermometer. It is ten degrees Fahrenheit. I groan. Not today! For today, Saturday, February 2, 1974, is sale day for the farm equipment and the farm. The cows, however, will not be auctioned off until Monday. We hurry through the morning chores. Breakfast goes down in a few gulps and then I am ready to slide my arms into a sweater, followed by three coats. I have slipped jeans on under my dress. Overall, I look like one of those stuffed scarecrows. I won't be able to move, but I am hoping that I will be warm. The sun has slid behind the clouds, and within an hour, it begins to rain. *What a miserable day for a sale.* In spite of the weather, the farm equipment sells well, and the day moves along well. Finally, it is time to auction off the farm. The crowd has thinned to a couple dozen people. Daddy has decided to place the farm up for bids, as there have been no acceptable offers through the real estate agency.

"Who will give me $200,000? Start this fine productive farm at $200,000," calls the auctioneer. His call is met by stony silence. "How about $150,000? Who will start out at $150,000?"

"I'll give you $130,000," shouts one not-quite-totally-frozen statue.

"Now, who will give me $150,000?"

No one moves. In spite of the auctioneer's continued urging, no one offers to increase the bid. This amount doesn't even begin to approach what Daddy is hoping for. Daddy shakes his head "no" to indicate that he is not selling today.

Beep, beep, beep! I roll over and rub my eyes. I search for the reason that this noise keeps intruding into my sleep-fogged brain. I squint at the clock. It is midnight. And then I remember; I need to get up and milk one last time. Hurrah! We are milking at midnight so that the cows' udders will be plump and nice-looking for the sale today. I stagger down the steps and out the door. The thermometer pronounces that this will be another cold day. I can see my breath in the frosty morning air as I walk to the barn under the starlit sky.

After breakfast, I pull on two sweaters this time, followed by the three coats. My job is to stand by the auctioneer's booth and hand the pedigree papers for each cow to the man who will read the information to the buyers. Grasping papers with gloved hands is impossible, it seems, and my hands are soon stiff and cold from the exposure. As the day wears on, the cold creeps through my protective inner layer. My feet become unfeeling blocks of ice. By the time the one-hundredth cow is sold, the cold has seeped deep into my bones. I am shaking fiercely, and my knees no longer bend.

The ice in our bones just adds to our huge disappointment with the day. The average market price for good dairy cows is $800, but we have barely gotten $600 apiece. It probably does not help that there is a truckers' strike in progress right now. The cows and other things we are not taking with us are gone, but their sale did not bring us the cash Daddy had hoped for, and the farm is

still not sold. We gather around the supper table after everyone
has left. Daddy is very quiet. His jaw muscles stretch like tight
bands, and his eyes are focused on the food on his plate. Everyone
eats in silence.

A month has passed. I awaken at six o'clock and, in a leisurely
way, dress for the day. Ah! It is so relaxing to dress slowly and eat
breakfast before going out. There are no cows to milk, no time
schedules to meet. In the place of milking, though, for the last
two weeks on Monday, Wednesday, and Friday, we have been
hauling hay out of our barn to an auction barn in southeastern
Pennsylvania. We are making early use of the 1966 Mack tractor-trailer Daddy recently bought to haul our farm machinery to
our new home in Minnesota. The man who bought the hay at
our sale has been unable to pay for it, so now it has become our
responsibility to move it. The man who bought the silage did not
pay for it either, but the defaulted buyer had already gotten it
before we found that he had no money. Not only did we lose the
money but we lost the silage as well. Between the days that we
have been hauling hay, Daddy and Paul have been shelling corn
from the crib to sell.

Daddy got up earlier today to take a load of shelled corn to
town. Paul and I take the canvas off the trailer load of hay that we
loaded last evening while we wait for Daddy's return. Paul is my
favorite brother, and I don't mind helping him. We are chums and
often gang up against Joseph. Besides, I love going along on these
trips to places I have never been, and it seems pretty cool to be
identified with the semi-truck-driving cowboys. This is definitely
not an acceptable identity for a Mennonite girl, but Daddy allows
it, and I take advantage of that consent. Daddy is the driver, Paul

gets the passenger's seat, and I get a spot in the sleeper section of the tractor cab. I don't care where I have to sit. I am just happy to go along because interestingly, Joseph, the other son, usually gets left at home.

"You would just stand around with your hands in your pockets anyway," Daddy digs at him.

Ka-bump, ka-bump, ka-bump goes the semi-tractor as we cross each segment of concrete on Interstate 90. I think this is the roughest road we have been on since we left Pennsylvania. We are now in Minnesota, and this is my first trip to see our new place.

Daddy and Paul made the first trip alone, leaving Pennsylvania on March 18. Since we only own a flatbed, Daddy had rented a drop-down trailer to move the 4430 John Deere tractor and Uni-System (combine). Joseph and I stayed at home with Mama. I busied myself with making dresses, helping to pack, and reading. One morning, when Joseph went out to feed the heifers, he found a wobbly legged calf. It seemed that one of the pregnant heifers we had kept decided to have her calf. Oh dear. I was unprepared for this, since we no longer have any milking equipment. I decided that the calf was probably the best milker around and left it to do the job.

Daddy and Paul returned four days later, on March 22, and began immediately loading for another trip.

"Please, can I go along this time?" I begged.

"You need to stay at home," was Daddy's stern response.

I was so disappointed. But for whatever reason, Daddy changed his mind at the last minute.

"If you can get up at three tomorrow morning, you can go along with us."

Daddy, Paul, and I leave at four o'clock in the morning on March 26. This trip, we are hauling the disk, the cultivator, the haybine, the husker bed, and the flail chopper—not to mention numerous smaller items. We drive all day, following the northern route, the toll way, through Pennsylvania, Ohio, Indiana, and Illinois. Daddy stops only long enough to refuel and to sleep for half an hour on the turnpike. We are exhausted by midnight when Daddy finally scopes out a motel in Janesville, Wisconsin. With weary bodies and visions of sweet sleep, we enter the room assigned to us. The floor is warm, which feels really good on the feet, but we soon realize that the room is ninety degrees and there seems to be no way to turn down the heat. We turn on the air conditioner, but that doesn't seem to provide much relief either. We spend the night in restless tossing as perspiration soaks the sheets. We drag our aching bodies and bleary eyes out to the truck in the morning and are on the road again by eight.

After rhythmically bumping more than one hundred miles into Minnesota, we pull into the farm yard of our new home around two in the afternoon. I am not exactly impressed. It is cloudy and dreary, and brown is the predominant color of the landscape. Mud is everywhere. The house and garage have no paint on their barren siding. A roofless clay-block silo rests beside the red wooden barn. A lone concrete stave silo stands at the head of a muddy feedlot. A couple of shabby outbuildings lean into the wind. In all this, the only thing that looks like it hasn't been around for a hundred years is the flat-roofed metal machine shed.

The seller is present, and we spend the rest of the afternoon lifting the items off the trailer with the help of his backhoe. We tuck as much as possible into the machine sheds to get it out of the weather. After a restless night, curled up to stay warm at Benjamin Penner's, the Mennonite man Mama wrote about during their scouting trip, we are up and going again by five. The plan is to drive to Moline, Illinois, today in the hope of obtaining a payload of new machinery from International Harvester or John Deere to haul back to Pennsylvania. We arrive in Moline by late morning, but Daddy is not having any success reaching anyone that is willing to give him a load. We sit in the truck at a truck stop while we wait. Daddy is finally told that maybe tomorrow there will be a load that he can haul east, so we decide to book a motel for the night. It feels good to have a cozy, warm bed for one night anyway. The next morning, while Paul and Daddy make an in-person trip to the International Company, I stay at the motel and watch *The Waltons* on TV. TV is not allowed in our house, so this is a special treat for me. Leaving me is not meant to be a treat though. I am left at the motel because Daddy thinks he has a better chance of getting a load if he doesn't reveal that he has a second passenger with him. But after several hours, they come back empty-handed—or should I say empty-trucked.

"Let's go," is Daddy's brisk command. "We've wasted enough time already."

Apparently, what Daddy is trying to do is seen as too high of a liability risk by everyone he contacts, or he just doesn't have the right permits. He is not really sure what the issue is. But, there is an urgency to move on so that we can complete the move to Minnesota as expediently as possible. Planting time is fast approaching, and a farmer knows he must be ready when the weather is.

The mudroom door bangs. Daddy stands in the dining room doorway of our Minnesota house.

"Another heifer had a calf since the cattle arrived. She must have had it last night."

This is not what I want to hear on our first day as a family together in Minnesota. Fifty-five head of calves and young heifers arrived by potbelly trailer twenty-four hours before we did. Daddy had made sure to include the already fresh one and several that looked close to calving on this load. The stress of the twenty-two hour ride without food and water must have triggered the birth. Now there are two first-calf heifers to milk by hand each morning and night, and that responsibility will fall to either Joseph or me.

Joseph and I must come up with a routine to get this task done. The old red barn is the only structure that is attached to the muddy feedlot and its adjoining open pasture. We just have to figure out how to get them through the small door leading into it. Joseph unenthusiastically plods after me, not at all interested in stomping through foot-deep mud. We end up clomping this way and that, waving arms and shouting, before we convince our two mamas that choosing the narrow doorway is a better decision than choosing the wide-open spaces. We must then corner them and tie them up with baler twine before beginning the task of dodging well-aimed kicks to relieve them of their milk. It wouldn't be so bad if these were well-trained cows, but they are first-time mamas and are not interested in having their teats pulled rhythmically by some human. Daddy's hope was that the heifers would not freshen until after the new barn was completed. The problem is that the barn is not even in the works yet. *I hope that this is the last of the fresh heifers for a while.*

Raindrops dribble on the roof, and fog hangs heavy over the land. Today, April 11, is our fourth day together in Minnesota. Grammy, Mama's seventy-something-year-old mother who accompanied us on our trip, and I spend the day scrubbing the remaining parts of the house. We have been scrubbing for three days straight, and it is finally starting to look livable. Esther Penner, the wifely half of the Mennonite couple that lives near Garvin, came to help us one day, which made the work go so much faster. Once the house is clean, we can start unloading all the boxes off the truck.

The sky is still pitch black the following morning as we drive down the lane and past the windbreak on our right, on our way back to Pennsylvania for still more possessions. This time, all six of us are packed into the Buick. We have left the Chevy farm truck in Minnesota permanently.

Mama, Grammy, Joseph, and I leave Daddy and Paul off in Bedford, Pennsylvania, where we have left the semi for repairs. They climb into the truck and turn west again while the rest of us continue heading east for what still feels like home to me. There, Grandpop is waiting to take Grammy back home to eastern Pennsylvania.

I dress hurriedly after rolling out of my floor bed at five thirty. Today, April 19, I am going with Daddy and Paul to Shamokin to get the cattle trailer that Daddy has rented. I am excited to be a part of this moving of the last cattle. Daddy was unable to hire someone for a reasonable price to haul the remaining heifers to Minnesota, so he has decided to haul them himself. The plan is to pack the top deck with boxes this afternoon and then get the cattle loaded by evening. Once the cattle are loaded, getting on the road is of priority.

By ten, we are back with the cattle trailer, and the loading of boxes begins. During the last week, Mama, Joseph, and I have secured all the boxes with baler twine and carried them from the attic, cellar, and spring house to the main floor of the house. Now, we just need to move them to the truck. One person grunts and pushes the boxes forward while the rest of us carry them out. Our arms and legs ache and are already becoming wobbly by the time we begin the equally labor-intensive task of loading the cattle. Trying to convince twenty frisky heifers that going up a ramp into a small hole is a good idea is not an easy chore. We shout and wave our arms. We push and shock with the cattle prod. We are soon covered with some not-so-pleasant material. After several hours of going around in circles, all the heifers are finally loaded. There is no time to sleep, though, as the cattle will already be on the trailer for twenty-two hours just for the drive alone. Daddy, Paul, and I pull out of the farm yard at eleven o'clock that night. Daddy's intent is to drive all night long, but after several hours, he is starting to swerve off to the side of the road at regular intervals. He stops twice at rest stops. The truck rocks back and forth, though, with the constant movement of the cattle. Sleep is impossible, so we drive on. In Wisconsin, we are pulled over by the State Patrol because we have no name or weight-limit signs on the doors of the truck. This delay adds twenty minutes to our journey.

It is dark again and approaching one in the morning before we exit the interstate and head out on county roads to the farm. Because it is spring in Minnesota, the roads are posted with weight-limit restrictions. No more than ten tons per axle is allowed. That means we are not supposed to be taking a loaded semi on any county roads. Hoping not to attract attention, Daddy turns off the truck lights. We rumble through the shadows under the moonlight. I feel like a character in one of those mystery novels I love to read, and goose bumps rise on my arms. We do arrive at our destination without being stopped or driving into the ditch. The mud underfoot has not diminished. We slip and slide through its cold wet clutches to finally release our captives. They have spent twenty-seven hours without food or water, squashed together in the confines of the metal cage. Once they are fed and watered, Daddy, Paul, and I crash into our beds. Since it is Sunday, we let sleep claim us for the whole day.

Daddy sits hunched at the phone, dialing number after number. It is Monday morning, and he is trying to book a payload of hogs for the return trip back East. He is told that there will be no pigs until tomorrow. I make my way to the barn and milk the two heifers that need such services. We do not have enough milk to sell, so we drink some and give some away to those helping us. The rest of the day is spent unloading the boxes from the top of the trailer and carrying them to the basement.

The call finally comes at noon on Tuesday. There is a load of hogs for pickup in southern Iowa. We are soon back on the road again, ka-bumping through Iowa. We arrive in Fairfield by eight that evening. One hundred seventy-four protesting pigs are prodded and pushed up the ramp and into the trailer. We are ready to roll by eleven. Now we have not only the constant rocking, but also high-pitched squeals and a pungent odor to accompany us. Every time we stop, the smell drifts forward and overwhelms us. Daddy drives through the night, the next day, and on into the next night with only a couple of rest stops. The transmission does not seem to be shifting right. I can feel the tension in the air as we all wonder the same thing: is the truck going to make it? It is two in the morning, twenty-seven hours after we left Fairfield, when we roll into Philadelphia. It is a good thing that it is the middle of the night because we have no idea where we are going. Daddy makes several wrong turns before we finally find the packing plant.

The plant is dark and deserted. Daddy crawls into the sleeper

and Paul and I each claim a seat to curl up in. We shut our eyes
and try to sleep to the rocking motion until the sun's rays begin
to brighten the sky, and the day's workers arrive. Getting the pigs
off the truck is almost as labor-intensive as getting them on. After
much squealing, pushing, and prodding, our load is finally on its
way to becoming someone's lunch, and we head for home.

Just six days after our return from the hog delivery, it is time
to travel the road that will make us officially Minnesotans. It is
close to midnight before we finish loading all the vehicles and pull
away from the house. It is too late to set out with our four-vehicle
caravan, so we travel about thirty miles, to the home of Edward
Hirschler, a fellow church member. There we spend the night.
The Hirschlers' home is convenient as a stopping place because
they live along our route to the turnpike. At seven thirty on the
morning of April 29, we wave good-bye to lifelong friends and
set out for our destination.

Daddy is leading with the semi, loaded with a bin, the skid
steer, and other things. Joseph is accompanying him. Paul is next
in line. He is driving the 1955 Ford farm truck, loaded with the
rest of our furniture, and seated beside him is our dog, Lady.
Behind him, I, at sixteen, am driving alone in our two-year-old
Ford pickup, which is loaded with barn equipment. I feel pretty
important to be trusted like this, as I have only had my driver's
license for about two months. Last in line is Mama. She is bringing up the rear with the Buick, loaded with the food and our
clothing changes.

I struggle to keep my eyes open and follow the truck ahead of me on the rain-slicked roads of the Chicago skyway. The white lines along the edge of the road blur in the glare of the oncoming traffic, while traffic traveling our direction whizzes by at breakneck speed. It is one o'clock in the morning. We have been driving for eighteen hours, and my eyes want to drift shut. I know that I am swerving. Paul is swerving from side to side ahead of me. I want to stop, but I can't, as there is no means of communication with the other vehicles. I just have to keep driving until Daddy decides to pull off.

"I want to get through Chicago at night. There is less traffic that way," was Daddy's communication to us earlier in the day.

Finally, around 2 a.m., Daddy pulls into the Clock Tower Inn at Rockford, Illinois. We are all dead tired and just want to collapse. We have a problem though. The motel does not want any animals in the room. We make a decision to leave Lady in the old Ford truck because we do not know what else to do with her. Lady is still a very young German Shepherd, not quite a year old, and now she is being left alone in an unfamiliar place. We come out the next morning to find tiny pieces of seat stuffing covering the floor and tumbling out the door. But Lady wags her tail furiously and jumps all over us.

Our caravan takes off in formation again, following I90 for the rest of the drive to Minnesota. I am still tired and my head nods all day in spite of my determination to stay awake. That old, peeling house looks pretty inviting when we roll up outside of it around three in the afternoon. I just want to flop in a chair, but the semi-trailer needs to be unloaded as quickly as possible. Dark clouds gathering in the west soon interrupt our project with a downpour. A flash of lightning follows. The lights blink, and then we are thrown into darkness. Daddy decides to call it a day and wait until tomorrow to finish.

The following morning, May 2, the sun has reappeared, along with the wind. It seems to always be windy here which is certainly advantageous for drying the ground. Daddy and Paul finish unloading the semi-trailer. Paul, Joseph, and I then unload the rest of the furniture and place it in the appropriate rooms while Daddy goes to town. Daddy is pushing to quickly make one last trip to Pennsylvania. The sun is shining, and May is the ideal time for planting corn and soybeans in Minnesota. But two of our tractors are still in Pennsylvania, and we need to get them quickly. The new corn planters we are buying are not ready yet either, but Daddy is hoping that they will have arrived by the time we return. This means that Daddy and I are back on the road for Pennsylvania by that afternoon. Paul is staying behind this time to prepare as much of the ground as possible for planting. Joseph will take care of the cattle.

We can no longer hear ourselves talk as the rumble of the truck gets louder. It is four days later, and we are making our way across Indiana on our return trip with the 4010 and 3010 John Deere tractors. Exhaust fumes begin to creep into the cab, making me want to hold my breath and not inhale. To top it off, it is night again, and cold and raining, but we need to keep the windows open to get fresh air. Daddy presses on as long as possible but finally stops at Allen's Corner in Hampshire, Illinois, at three in the morning. We just can't go on like this anymore. While we wait for morning light, we try to sleep. But running the truck for heat is not an option, and the cold seeps in, driving any thought of sleep away.

The diagnosis of the mechanic when he arrives for work at six is that the manifold gaskets are bad. But we came to the right place, and they get the truck right into the shop. The repairs are completed with speed and efficiency, and we are on our way by ten in the morning. I am only too happy to be greeted by the ka-bump, ka-bump, ka-bump that announces our arrival in Minnesota. By late afternoon, we are making the last turn into our driveway. We are greeted by the sight of flying dust in the neighboring fields and tractors methodically making their way up and down the fields. This is home now, and I think I have had enough adventure on the road to satisfy me for a while. Our next projects are to get the crops planted and the dairy barn built.

Chapter 3

THE FIRST YEAR

I stare out the window at the dark clouds and the drizzle that drips from them. I shiver. The last couple of weeks have been a repeating pattern of cool, cloudy, rainy days. The end of May is only a few days away. Daddy is very anxious to get the crops planted, but we have not been able to get into the fields to plant anything. We were making the last trip to Pennsylvania during the one nice week at the beginning of May while other farmers were planting as fast as they could go. Not only were we still in the midst of moving, we did not have all the equipment needed to do the job. Last week, the corn planters were finally delivered. There are two six-row planters hooked together with a bar, creating a humongous twelve-row planter. The plan is to pull the corn planter with the 4010 John Deere and to use the 4430 for working ground and putting anhydrous ammonia on for nitrogen.

My feet hit the floor at 5:00 a.m. in response to the beep, beep, beep of the alarm clock. The bathroom in this house also shares a wall with Joseph's bedroom, and I again start the routine that will become part of our lives for the next ten years. Knock, knock, knock on the bathroom wall to arouse Joseph from sleep. I need his help to catch the two heifers that need to be milked by hand. In my mind, this just isn't a very efficient way to milk cows, but for right now there is no other choice. We each hand-milk one heifer and feed the milk to the calves and stray cats.

By six thirty, I ride my bike back to the house and hurry to make breakfast. Mama has started a new job here, working nights as a nurse at the local hospital twenty miles from the farm. The task of making the dreaded oatmeal now falls to me. Daddy and Paul are working on the corn planter, making sure everything is in order—with the hopes of planting later today. Joseph is expected to feed the heifers and calves before he comes in to breakfast. There is no silo unloader, so he has to fork the silage out by hand and then wheel it out to the heifers with the wheelbarrow. Because everyone is busy, we have stopped eating breakfast together. Everyone eats when it suits him or her.

Daddy soon comes into the kitchen to talk to me.

"I want you to take the truck to town for fertilizer as soon as you are done with breakfast."

"Okay," I nod. I quickly wash my shoofly pie down with my cocoa, leaving my dirty dishes for Mama to wash after she gets home.

Daddy has bought a gravity box and chained it to the bed of the 1965 Chevy truck. This we will fill with bulk fertilizer from the elevator in town. To unload it, one needs to turn the wheel that opens the gate, and the fertilizer then runs out, into an auger that will carry it to the fertilizer boxes on the planters. This is much easier than buying it in bags and loading the planter by hand, one bag at a time. I am feeling pretty grown-up and important as I head out to town alone to get the fertilizer.

By the time I return, Daddy and Paul have the corn planters ready. We load the bagged seed corn unto the truck and head for the field. Heavy black clods stick to the tractor tires, but in spite of the dampness, we begin planting. Paul discs the ground ahead of the planter while Daddy puts the seed in the ground. Joseph and I man the fertilizer truck and help reload the seed corn. As we sit in the truck and watch, the green tractor fades into the distance before the speck turns around and begins to grow larger again. Our Minnesota fields are so large they seem to have no end. This one is over three-quarters of a mile long. Because of the wet soil conditions, some of the rows make half circle detours around the wet spots. It has begun to look like an earthworm has slithered over the black earth.

Daddy has barely planted fifty acres of corn on our first day of planting when the western sky begins to darken. Within thirty minutes, storm clouds roll in, and the wind picks up. Daddy has just made his turn at the other end of the field and started back toward us. The sky grows darker and darker. Daddy is still just a growing spec in the distance when the heavens release their torrents. Perspective is lost in the driving rain and Daddy drives right into a wet spot instead of around it. He becomes stuck in the thick goo. The tractor and planter are abandoned until the next day and everybody runs for cover. This day becomes a repeating pattern over the next couple of weeks as we struggle between rain and wet soil to get the corn into the ground.

Sundays are designated as a day of rest in our faith and in our family. Only work that is absolutely necessary is to be done. Therefore, Sunday is a welcome day of diversion. To this day, a little scolding finger still wags back and forth in my head when I observe Christian farmers planting or harvesting on Sundays.

There are four Mennonite families (of which we are one) now living in this area, and the hope is to be able to encourage enough new families to move into the area that a new community can be established. We are meeting in each other's homes for services until a permanent church building can be found. The minister, Peter Wiehler, and his wife have eight children, four of whom fall between the ages of sixteen and twenty-one. I am delighted by this, as I have never really had any close Mennonite friends. In Pennsylvania, we lived some distance from the Mennonite community we belonged to, and I never was able to spend any time with other young people my age in the faith. Our families mesh together well. Paul soon develops a strong friendship with Andrew, while Donna and Nancy take me under their wing.

Today, we will meet at Benjamin Penner's for the worship service. Because the families are scattered over a seventy-mile radius, services are scheduled for one o'clock in the afternoon rather than the traditional morning time. I listen to music on the radio in my room, read some, and then take a nap until we are ready to leave for the fifteen-mile trip to the Penners' house. Upon arrival there, twenty of us gather in the living room for the a cappella singing of hymns followed by a scriptural message by Peter. Food and fellowship follow the service.

"Andrew, Donna, and I need to take off. We need to take a pickup back to Chiland (Wisconsin) and pick up Nancy to get her moved to Minnesota too," Jacob Wiehler announces after lunch. "We borrowed the pickup to move some of our stuff from there."

He turns to Paul and me.

"Do you guys want to go along for the ride?"

My face lights up. That would be a resounding yes. This sounds like fun to me, and I am excited. This move to Minnesota has it perks, and I like the new experiences this adventure has brought to my life.

The afternoon passes far too quickly as chatter and laughter fill the drive over and home again. We stop at a lock and dam on the Mississippi River to watch a tug push some barges through. Splurging on an ice-cream treat is also a necessity. By the time the Wiehlers drop us off at home, the sun is sinking into a cloud bank of red streaks. It has been a stimulating day, but tomorrow we must get back to the business of planting.

The weather has turned hot and humid. The calendar is entering the last week of June, and we have just finished planting corn between the rain showers. The last four weeks have been filled with many additional tasks besides the planting. Plans have been finalized for the new parlor and free-stall barn, which will be built yet this summer. This is not a minute too soon for me, as a third heifer has had her calf. I am starting to feel a bit overwhelmed by the hand-milking experience. There has been a garden to tend and we had to paint the house. Grandpop and Grammy drove out the week of June 7, and Joseph and I helped them scrape and paint for a week. The house does look nice now with its clean white coat.

We have spent this last week of June primarily planting soybeans. This morning after milking, I climb into the cab of the 4430 John Deere tractor to work ground. Paul is mowing hay while Daddy finishes planting. This is the only tractor with a cab, so I feel privileged to get to use it. I will stay clean and cool while the menfolk get hot and dirty. It also gives me a feeling of power to sit up high above the earth and go endlessly around and around. Working ground leaves unlimited amounts of time for daydreaming. Little brain power is needed to keep the tractor on its path for the fifteen to twenty minutes before the end of the field appears and I need to turn around. Sometimes I almost fall asleep. The trick is to wake up long enough to get turned around before tearing out an electric pole or tree or fence post at the end of a row.

On this hot, breezy early July morning, the hay Paul cut yesterday is already dry, and we switch to putting up hay. Daddy bales and Paul brings the hay wagons to the barn. We have a "kicker" baler, so we do not stack the bales on the wagon. Instead, they just land inside the high side boards skewed every which way. This does make for a challenge when unloading, though. The unloading person tugs and pulls to remove the bottom bales until the upper ones come cascading down—sometimes on the unprepared head of a person underneath. The more difficult job, though, is stacking the hay in the haymow, as it is stifling in the cramped quarters of the barn. Joseph and I usually get this job while Paul unloads and places the bales on the elevator to come up to us. Paul does not have a slow or even semi-slow gear, so the bales come up in rapid fire succession. I wear jeans under my dress to protect my legs from the hay stubble, and I am soon soaked in perspiration from the fast pace in this stuffy heat. By evening, I don't think I can move another muscle, as we have baled ten acres of hay and put away twelve hundred bales. I am exhausted and on the verge of collapse. I am looking forward to my bed. But being able to sleep will be tricky tonight, as there is no air conditioning in our house. Sometimes, I turn crossways on the bed and lay my head by the open window in the hope that there might be a slight breeze to cool my wet forehead and allow sleep to come.

The constant rains have finally moved on, leaving hot, dry weather in their wake. We have spent the month of July making hay every few days. And there are the three heifers to milk by hand each morning and evening. This morning, July 24, when I went out to do the milking, there stood another excited mother with a wobbly legged calf. *No! Not another one to milk by hand.* The new milking barn hasn't even been started yet. This is not how I planned to spend my summer—milking a dozen animals by hand.

"You need to do something. This is just impossible. I can't keep milking all these animals by hand," I implore Daddy.

To my surprise, he agrees with me. Together we make a trip to the local Delaval dealer, who is happy to sell us two old Surge bucket milk machines and an old vacuum pump. We place the vacuum pump in the feed room by the old silo and Daddy spends the day running vacuum pipe above the little stall area where we have been tying our bossies for hand milking. He finishes up by wiring the little system. I am delighted. *This should make things a little easier.* The only issue now is that our little herd has never seen or heard a milking machine before, and they are not convinced that this is a better idea. Ears twitch at the new sounds, feet brace, and extra pushing and prodding is needed to get them into the milking area. This is followed by a few well-placed kicks, a clattering of buckets, and more frightened animals before the first milking is done this modern way. I sigh as I inspect my new bruises. This is definitely easier on the hands but certainly not easier or faster overall. Besides the angst of the animals, there are milk machines to wash and care for. We lug the heavy machines to the house and wash them in the big tubs that Mama uses for washing our clothes with the wringer washer. Since four cows will not produce enough milk to sell, Daddy decrees that we should make butter out of any milk that is not needed for the calves.

It is early August. Daddy has decided that since there is a lull in the farm work, it is time to make one last trip to Pennsylvania for some non-essential items. We left these items due to the urgency to get the crops planted here in Minnesota. The farm has still not been sold, and the place is vacant except for our things. There did not seem to be any need to hurry to finish up the moving.

Always up for an adventure, I beg to go along, and so it is that Daddy, Paul, and I climb into the cab of the semi early one morning and head out. Joseph is left at home, as usual, with Mama to milk the four cows and take care of the livestock. We arrive at the home of our Mennonite friend Edward Hirschler by mid-afternoon the next day. They feed the hungry travelers and loan us a car to drive out to the farm. The sight that greets us is a shock. The latch on the back door of the house has been broken, and most of the things that we left are gone. Our garden rototiller, my tricycle, Paul's pedal tractor, and numerous antique furniture pieces are missing. A fifty-gallon drum of fuel oil which Daddy had planned to use for our return trip is gone as well, along with a stack of sheet metal that had been tucked away in the barn. The concrete feed bunk is about the only thing that remains that isn't fastened down—and that is probably because it is too heavy to move easily. Exhausted and discouraged, we return to the Hirschlers' for the night.

Daddy has decided to sell the feed bunk instead of taking it to Minnesota as he had originally planned. We spend the next day moving it to its new home with the help of a neighbor's backhoe. We then load whatever we can find that is left on the trailer and are ready to head for home by late afternoon—or so we think. Daddy gets into the truck to start it, but the key isn't in the ignition. Pockets are emptied several times and the ground around the truck is scoured, but the key is nowhere to be found.

"Give me one of your bobby pins," Daddy instructs me. *Bobby pin? How is that going to help?* Nevertheless, I hand over one of my precious pins. Lo and behold, he inserts it into the ignition. Before long, we hear the welcome rumble of the engine, and we are off. There will be no turning the truck off until we get home.

We arrive home at six thirty the following evening, Sunday, August 11. We are all very tired and grouchy. To top everything off, I find out that two more heifers have had calves while we were gone, making six cows to milk now in our primitive milking setup. I feel like nothing is right in my world.

The manure pit floor was poured two weeks ago, and today, the crane is here to lift the pit sides and slatted floor into place. At least we are making some visible progress on the barn. It has been two weeks since our return from Pennsylvania, and every couple of days now, a new calf is born. I go out to check on the heifers today and see just one little foot sticking out of one heifer. A calf cannot be born if both feet and the nose are not coming together, so something needs to be done. Daddy is not around, so I decide to try to fix the problem myself. I wash my arms and grab some baler twine, and I sneak up behind the laboring animal. I have never tried this before, but I have watched the vet a few times. I reach in and feel for the foot that is missing. I figure that all I have to do is push it back and flip it around. That obviously is easier said than done, as every time I push back on the slippery leg, the animal gives a huge heave and the leg goes right back where it was. After rolling belly down in the dirt for some time, I am finally successful, and both feet come popping out. I fasten the baler twine around both ankles, sit on the ground, prop my feet on the back of the cow, and pull with each one of her mighty pushes. Soon, I have a slippery, sloppy calf in my lap. I feel a sense of satisfaction with my achievement. Watching the first moments of a new, fresh life is exciting and wonderful. I do not know it yet, but today is the beginning of what will become one of my primary roles in working with our dairy cows—their health care.

There are now twenty-two cows to milk and fifteen heifer calves to feed by bucket. We have graduated from making butter with the milk to shipping it in cans to a local Grade B cheese factory. The addition of a chain around the neck of each animal has at least given us a handle to grab onto when an animal wishes to be uncooperative. Each milking, we chase them, two by two, into our little wooden box stall, fasten them with baler twine to the wooden plank, and place the milkers on. Between each change of cow couples, the milk is emptied into a large stainless steel strainer, from which the milk trickles into a milk can. Once the can is full, Joseph rolls it out to the cattle water tank, where the two of us together heave the eighty pound can into the tank. The water is cool and will keep the milk from spoiling before it is picked up the following morning. It takes us sometimes three to four hours to get through the milking and feeding. The whole operation is one of mass chaos, primarily because all of these animals are first-time cows who are not the least bit interested in cooperating without significant physical persuasion from us. Daddy and Paul rarely help, as they see this area as Joseph's and my responsibility. We are left to struggle alone. Sometimes I am in tears by the time we are done because this is so frustrating and hard, and there is little support for our predicament. Daddy usually just sets his jaw and walks away when I am emotional. This only increases my perception that I am not being listened to—that how I feel doesn't really matter

to him. But I persevere because I know that once the barn is
built, the milking will be easier.

Contact on Sundays with the other families of the small
Mennonite group in Minnesota brighten my world and provide
respite from the workaday world. The group, however, is finding
it a challenge to find a central place for worship. The families
already in Minnesota before we arrived had rented a Moravian
Church building to hold services in; it is about fifty miles from
our farm. The lease has expired, and the group feels it is time to
look for a building that will provide a more central meeting point
with a definite time for worship. Over the course of the last several
months, a couple of different buildings have been pursued. The
first one that came to the attention of the men was a church building that was vacated when two protestant churches combined. It
is in the town nine miles north of the farm. It had been on the
market for quite some time. The men approached the trustees of
the church with the intent of making the purchase. They were
bitterly disappointed to learn that one of the trustees had already
sold the building to a man for a house—without the knowledge
of the other trustees.

There was another little white church building fifteen miles
away to the west of our place that had been closed for thirty
years. The men thought it might suit our purposes. It just needed
a little updating. A potbelly wood-burning stove graced the
corner, gas lights hung from the ceiling, and the bell pealed
out a lovely sound when the rope was pulled. An old Swedish
Bible and hymn books were lying in their intended places, and
the foot-operated organ was silently waiting for someone to put
its keys in motion. It was in a lovely, quiet country setting with

a small cemetery. There were only six living members left, who were well into their sixties and seventies, and they met only once a year to clean the building. When approached about selling the building, they were willing to do so—but only if our group would agree to move it away from the cemetery. The building could hardly stand such a drastic move, so it was with more disappointment that the men decided it was necessary to keep looking. So for the time being, our four families will continue to meet in our homes for worship.

The friendship of Andrew, Jacob, Nancy, Michael, and Donna Wiehler, especially, meets a need for Paul, Joseph, and me that has never been met before. Paul and I are, therefore, delighted by an invitation to join Nancy, Andrew, and Michael on a weekend trip to Dell Rapids, Wisconsin, in late August. The Dell Rapids Mennonite Church is having special services this particular weekend, and the Wiehler children really want to attend. Daddy agrees to give us this break, and he and Joseph stay home to handle the chores. By noon on Saturday, Paul and I are cruising down interstate 90 in Dad's Ford pickup with our destination being Peter Wiehler's farm. It is about an hour's drive from our place. There, we transfer to the Wiehlers' car. The stress of the last few weeks melts away as laughter takes its place. The five of us joke, laugh, and share chitchat during our six-hour ride. The Wiehlers have relatives at Dell Rapids, and, in good Mennonite tradition, we are fed a hearty supper at their uncle's home upon our arrival. Then Nancy and I are taken to one of the minister's homes for the night's lodging. Six other young ladies are already gathered there. Besides hosting the visitors, Walter Thiessen and his wife have eight daughters and one son. I do not know any of the guests except Nancy. I am not sure how to act in this environment, as none of us children has been allowed to spend time with other families during our teen years before now.

I have no experience with spending time away from my family. I feel very self-conscious, and my stomach is churning with anxiety. I look forward to trying these new experiences, but then when I get there, I feel very awkward. The only thing I really know how to do properly is work. Maybe that's why the routine of the farm is comforting.

I crawl out of my sleeping bag on the floor the next morning, Sunday, to the smell of pancakes. The house is a beehive of activity as everyone gets ready for church. Mrs. Thiessen is cooking a hearty breakfast of pancakes, eggs, and applesauce. The older girls are busy helping the younger ones get dressed and braiding their hair. Before long, Walter and his son come in from milking the cows, and all nineteen of us sit down to eat. Walter, in his role as head of the family, reads scripture from the Bible for a devotional time and says grace before everyone reaches for the food. I soon discover that I don't need to worry much about needing to talk, as I am basically just another spot at the table and pretty much unnoticed. Nancy talks for both of us when the questions are directed our way. That suits me just fine. After breakfast, the dishes are quickly done, and we are soon out the door. The church is just down the road, less than a mile away. We enjoy a sun-drenched, leisurely walk there.

There are three services scheduled for the day. Each service starts out with a couple of hymns sung in four-part a cappella by the congregation. The singing is followed by one or two messages. There is a break at noon, and we are all invited to eat dinner at the home of one of the other families. Then we return for the afternoon service, which follows the same pattern as the morning one. During the break between the afternoon and evening service, the Wiehlers take us to their uncle's home for ice cream and a tour of the community. Before I know it, it is time for the evening service. This pattern follows quite closely that of special all-day services I remember from the church we belonged to in Pennsylvania, and I find the familiarity comforting.

Sunday night, we all sleep at the home of Jay Fellman, another relative of the Wiehlers. I do not need to roll out until seven on Monday morning. Ah! What a luxury. Life is relaxed here, and no one seems to be in a hurry. I am envious of this pace. We finally close our overnight bags around nine thirty and head back to Minnesota. We talk about the weekend, laugh, and get silly as teenagers are prone to do. Way too soon, we are sitting at Brenda Wiehler's table, enjoying a late dinner. Then it is time to return to the farm and take over the milking of the cows again, the number of which is up to twenty-five. Paul and I dash upstairs to change clothes on our arrival home in mid-afternoon.

I shiver as I make my way to the barn in the early predawn morning. The thermometer says it is below freezing, and the wind whistles through the cracks of the barn boards. It is the third of October. The month of September has fled into the past. Our first light frost came on September 3, the night after Paul's and my return from Wisconsin, followed by a killing frost on September 22. The local folks tell us that this is early even for Minnesota. We were late with planting, so this is a huge blow to us. The crops are not at all mature. Only time will tell how much loss of yield has been sustained.

I glance over at the new milking setup that is rising from the ground. The new buildings cannot get done soon enough for me. The manure pit with its slatted floor is complete, and the main free-stall barn supports and trusses are up. The footer for the parlor was poured in early September, followed by the laying of the block to make the walls. Today, the builders are working on putting on the parlor roof.

My fingers are numb by the time I get the milkers together and begin my morning ritual. Snuggling up close between the warm bodies of the two cows whose udders I have attached the milk machines is the only thing that keeps me from freezing. I do this fourteen times over, as we have now increased in number to twenty-nine producing animals in this makeshift primitive setup. I cannot wait until the new barn is done. However, even in the archaic setup, things have fallen into a more hopeful routine, and by nine in the morning, the cows have once again been relieved of their full udders.

I eat a hurried breakfast because Daddy has said that I am needed today to drive the truck to chop corn silage onto. I love driving the truck. The responsibility it entails gives me a sense of being grown-up and equal to the adults in the world. Two weeks ago, Daddy bought a new Field Queen to chop the corn with which we will feed the cows through the winter. It is a bright-yellow self-propelled overgrown machine with a cab, and it is designed only for chopping. Pulling a wagon behind the chopper, he will alternate filling the two new green silage wagons, with their fancy unloading chains and beaters that arrived last week. At least that was the plan, but the first day of chopping resulted in both wagons breaking down. They are repaired, but they break over and over again. It is soon obvious that new chains will need to be ordered. Daddy is quite frustrated because we need to keep moving if we are going to get the harvesting done. Daddy has resorted to plan B, which is to have someone drive along beside him with the farm truck while he chops into it. The silage is then dumped onto a pile which Paul pushes, stacks, and packs down with the backhoe tractor.

I put the truck in second gear and try to match my pace to the speed of the chopper. The problem is that I cannot see the Field Queen operator from the driver's seat of the truck. It is only an educated guess, then, as to where the silage is actually landing. But with a little practice, I alternatively speed up and slow down in an effort to distribute the flying silage evenly onto the truck bed. When Daddy is too unhappy with the final landing place of our product or the truck is full, he blows the horn, and I stop so I can hop out of the truck and climb the steps to his haven to receive more specific, detailed instructions. Once the truck is full, I drive to where Paul is piling and trade my full truck for an empty one. Then it is back to the field for another load. By noon, Paul comes to inform Daddy that the backhoe has broken down, and he needs Daddy to go for parts. While Daddy goes to town, Paul takes over chopping the next two loads. Now I really have to pay attention, as speed is the name of the game when Paul drives anything. But then Paul is not nearly so particular as to whether it all lands on the truck or not.

I usually try to do things the way Daddy wants because I want him to be happy with me. Joseph doesn't seem to care because he can't ever do anything that Daddy is satisfied with anyway, and Paul seems to be able to do whatever he wants and not get reprimanded. I have always been aware of this dynamic but never thought much of it because it has always been this way. By the time Daddy is back from town with the parts, we have the two trucks loaded, and it is time for me to go attend to the cows for the evening milking.

A month has passed, and all the corn that we might possibly need for the cows and heifers has been chopped and piled or blown into our two silos. Daddy chose to chop the corn that most obviously had not matured, in the hope of keeping the more mature corn for combining and cash sale.

The first week of October brought the delivery of the corn dryer. It is a huge red machine, about twenty-five feet tall by fifty feet long. On one end is a burner fed by LP gas that generates the heat for drying the corn. The top section has a fan that pushes the heat back into the drying chamber, while the bottom section has a cooling fan. Corn is fed into the machine through a series of augers that take it to the top; then the corn falls down both sides of the dryer during the drying and cooling process. Finally, when it is dry enough, it is augered out the bottom and onto a waiting truck.

The delivery of the dryer was followed a few days later by the new John Deere combine. Just a few weeks before, a big four-wheel-drive workhorse of a tractor, a 7520, was delivered as well. "Nothing runs like a Deere" goes the slogan, and Daddy obviously believes this because we are proud of our John Deere equipment. The header on the combine is big enough to harvest six rows of crop at a time. In comparison to our combine in Pennsylvania, this one looks huge.

Since soybeans are particularly prone to absorbing moisture from wet weather, Daddy gives priority to combining the beans during a dry stretch of weather in mid-October. We only have about two hundred acres of soybeans to harvest, and the crop is poor. Ten bushels per acre seems to be the yield, while the normal is forty to fifty bushels per acre. We did not get the crop planted until late June, and then, with the early frost, the growing season was cut short by at least six to eight weeks. Not only is the yield low, the moisture is high. This means we will need to run them through the dryer, something that usually is not necessary.

Today, November 7, running the soybeans through the dryer is the order of the day. We fill the dryer with the beans and fire it up. Starting the dryer requires going through the correct series of button-pushing and switch-flipping until the high whine of the fans drowns out all other sounds. The experience has to be similar to standing behind a jet engine. As the crop comes out the bottom augers, Paul and I check the moisture using a special instrument. The goal is to get the moisture into the 10 to 12 percent range so that the soybeans won't spoil in the bin while being stored over the winter. But beans cannot be heated for long periods of time without splitting or otherwise being damaged. This means we must put them through three times before they are the correct moisture and are ready to be augured up into the one, small, thousand-bushel grain bin that we have. Sadly, that bin holds the entire soybean crop for the year.

I spend the day checking the moisture every thirty minutes and making adjustments on the speed that the beans are coming through the dryer to optimize the drying process. The small nuggets dribble into the Chevy truck bed until the pile becomes a mound that slides toward the sideboards. I pull the full truck away and replace it with the Ford before too much runs onto the ground. Joseph backs the loaded truck up to the dryer to empty the beans back into the dryer for the next drying run. If the soybeans are dry enough, he empties them into the bin for storage. The dryer can pretty much run by itself with minimal watching, so coordinating two jobs becomes standard procedure. I begin the milking a little early so that I can milk for a while, then go check on the dryer and move a truck if necessary, then go back to milking. Since the dryer is only about one hundred feet away from the milking operation, it is a workable process.

The weather has taken a definite turn toward winter by the following week. Snow is coming down, and the air is frigid when

I step off the cement steps into the darkness on the morning of
November 13. The barn building project is moving along, but
the parlor is still not ready to use for milking. Painting the milk
house ceiling and walls is the next order of business, and I spend
the day dedicated to this task until milking time comes around
again. Milking in our shanty and emptying the milk into cans
outdoors in this weather is torture for Joseph and me. The cows'
teats are becoming chapped and sore from the constant exposure
to the elements as well. The main free-stall barn is completed, so
Daddy decides this evening that we need to put the animals inside
the barn even if we can't use the parlor yet. Trying to get cows
to go into a new building on a bright sunny day is a huge task in
itself, but we are trying to do this in the dark and the cold. Daddy,
Paul, Joseph, and I spend three hours running around, waving
our arms and shouting at frisky black-and-white creatures who
would rather kick up their heels than go into a new place. We
end up, as well, doing what we so often do now when everyone
is stressed and upset. We sling words such as "you're so stupid,"
"don't just stand there," and "you're just not trying," mainly at
Joseph, who responds in a manner that makes the words ring true.
Sometimes, I participate in this name-calling. I suppose it lessens
the frustration with life if it's someone's fault when things don't
go well. I really don't think much about it at this point, as I am
simply following Dad and Paul's example. It is midnight when I
finally fall, exhausted, into bed. At least, I go to sleep knowing
that thirty animals are safely tucked in the barn away from old
man winter. It will be another week before we can actually start
milking in the new parlor, but we have made one more step in
that direction.

The Delaval milking equipment company technicians are on
schedule as they prepare to make the final push to completion.
They came today with the plan to be milking in the new barn by

evening. I am full of anticipation as Joseph and I struggle, hopefully for one last time, to bring the cows from their shelter in the new barn to the old barn for milking and then back again. The ground is now frozen and the milk cans have started to freeze into the water tank during the night after the warm milk direct from the cows has cooled.

After breakfast, I hurry back out to the barn to watch the progress. I finish some touch-up painting on the doors and clean up pieces of garbage left by the electrician and other workers. By seven o'clock in the evening, the bellowing of the cows lets us know that they are distressed about not being milked in a timely manner. But there are still a couple of hours of work left to be done. Finally, everything checks out, and the vacuum pump motor is humming. We open the parlor doors on both sides.

"Come on, bossies. Come on in here," we coax, holding out a bucket of grain. A few tentative steps, and the first ones venture into the bright, shiny new setup.

There are six stalls on each side in what is called a herringbone setup. This means the animals partially overlap as they stand alongside each other. Only the udders are lined up over the pit for the milker to access. All of the animals are skittish and jumpy. Not only are they in a new environment, they are not used to humans reaching up under them with no warning first. My first attempt to put a milker on results in a swift kick. It makes contact with the milker support arm that I have just extended under the unsuspecting animal. I see a flash of light and my world spins from the impact. As I touch my face, I see red spreading between my fingers. The cut on my lower lip extends all the way through. A trip to the house is necessary so that Mama can patch me up. I am embarrassed that all these men have seen me be the first casualty, but I am determined that this will not stop me. I am just as good as any of the men. I return to the fray.

Not all the animals are as agreeable as the first bunch. There is plenty of pushing, and prodding, and shocking, and shouting, until each animal makes that first step into the parlor. But with only thirty cows total and twelve spots for each rotation, it takes only two and one half changes, and we are all done. I can't believe how fast and slick this is.

Though the cattle are now in their new quarters, much of the corn is still in the field awaiting harvest. Daddy has been trying to combine corn for a couple of weeks already, but it is very slow going. Because the frost came before the corn was mature, most of it is very high in moisture. This has resulted in getting more mush than shelled corn into the combine bin.

Joseph and I get out of bed a little later today, November 26, and have the cows milked in an hour's time. Daddy is already out trying to combine, the dryer is running, and Paul is plowing. Throughout the day, I scurry back and forth from the dryer to the milk house office where we test the corn. The harvested corn is plump and squishy and tests at 40 percent moisture. Moisture checks need to be done every hour to make sure the drying corn is getting down to the desired 14 or 15 percent. But what I collect from the dryer outlet auger to test looks more like corn flakes then kernels of corn. I can hold the flakes in my hand and with a puff of wind, they blow away. As each truck loads with the dry flakes, it is taken to the flat-roofed metal shed and piled inside for storage. The "fruit of our labors" is pathetic.

By afternoon, it is snowing. Daddy has decided to return to chopping the corn for silage and to chop as much of the corn as possible in the next couple of days. He will leave the rest standing in the field until spring in the hope that it will air-dry enough that it can be combined for cattle feed. It is now obvious that most of our corn will not be acceptable for sale due to its low bushel weight. As a result, Daddy makes an executive decision to increase the dairy cattle numbers. There is no discussion with us about what we think needs to be done. Daddy is the boss, and he has always made the decisions alone. I am distressed by this turn of events, and I verbally protest his decision.

"You promised when we moved out here that we wouldn't milk more than fifty cows."

"That was before I knew we were going to have a crop failure. This is what we have to do to make a go of it."

Silently, I turn away. My feelings do not matter.

Paul definitely doesn't want to milk more cows either, but our voices go unheard. Mama encourages us to "do what you father says." I suspect that Mama really gets no input either, and she seems to be just fine with that. The seeds of discontent that have been planted in our first year are beginning to sprout, but neither Daddy nor I recognize them for the trees they will become. Any unhappiness regarding this decision needs to be suppressed, as I really have no say in the decision, and that is the way it is.

Daddy wastes no time in following through on his decision. Over the next couple of weeks, he buys two more small dairy herds of sixteen cows each and adds them to our current numbers. Within a month of moving into the new setup, our herd has increased to sixty cows.

On the last day of our first year in Minnesota, I write in my diary, "I wish I could disappear from here. If we had only stayed in Pennsylvania, maybe we could get along. We have to do all the giving and he's (Daddy) worse than ever. Once I said there was no (generation) gap but now I wonder." I am mostly confused, and I don't understand why my father is changing and what is driving his behavior. I do love farming, but I am tired of working all the time. I love working with the cows and seeing the new calves shake their heads to clear the cobwebs as they face a new world. I love the outdoors, watching the crops grow, and bringing in the fruit of the harvest. I just wish we didn't have to spend every hour of every day doing it. But then I unconsciously decide that, maybe if we all work harder and do the best we can in the short term, things will get easier once we have a few good years under our belt. All I need to keep going is hope that things will get better if I hang in there.

Chapter 4

YEAR TWO—THE YEAR OF DEDICATION WITH INCREASING DOUBT

*P*aul and Joseph show no interest in milking or caring for the dairy cows, so this becomes my domain. I see this as an area of specialty where I can concentrate my efforts and build approval from Daddy. I fall naturally into caring for the animals, and it is soon apparent that caring for numerous sick animals will require most of my time during our first winter in Minnesota. I really enjoy the health-care work—making the animals feel better. I even begin to entertain fleeting thoughts of going to Graham School, an advanced school for dairymen, in Garnett, Kansas, to get a degree.

Brr! The mercury is positioned at five degrees below zero on this January morning in 1975. I knock on the bedroom wall to arouse Joseph before I stumble downstairs at my usual time in the morning and slip my arms into my chore coat. Daddy is already out at the barn and chasing the first group of cows around into the holding area for milking. This leaves part of the stall area empty until the cows start to trickle back out through the parlor. During the time that the stall area has no cows, Joseph is expected to scrape the stall mats clean of any manure that has been dragged onto them during the night. Paul will not show up until later to help with cleanup. I set about placing the filter into the milk line to catch any dirt that might get into the milk, and I pluck the milking machines off of their wash racks. Lastly, I switch the milk delivery pipe in the milk house from the wash tub over to the milk tank. Then I flip the switch to awaken the vacuum pumps. I turn and double-check the pipe to make sure I have actually switched it over. Last week, we had milked several groups of cows before a trip into the milk house revealed a white river slowly coursing toward the drain and into the manure pit. *Oh no!* With a mad dash, I grabbed the pipe and swung it toward the tank, but not before another dump of the holding jar sent milk spewing all over the tank and milk house. Daddy's face darkened into a scowl when he discovered our forgetfulness.

"We don't have any money as it is, then you run what we do have down the drain."

I was crushed that he would insinuate that we did this on purpose. I want my father to be proud of me and believe in me. I am doing the best that I know how, and sometimes I make mistakes. I just wish he would be understanding and forgiving once in a while.

The milking machines need to be set up with everything ready to go by the time Daddy gets the cows packed in. We now have around one hundred cows to milk. Daddy went just last week and bought an additional thirty-one cows to add to our herd. I am exasperated with each new purchase of cows, but of course, my protests fall on deaf ears. Daddy has made his decision, and his decision is not open to discussion.

Daddy comes into the parlor carrying a hairless, calf-shaped blob. I know instantly that another pregnant cow has lost her calf. We have had numerous cows abort due to a disease called leptospirosis. Even though we have vaccinated all the cows, we are still losing calves. Cows that do not carry to term do not produce as much milk as cows who deliver at full term. A number of the cows are also running fevers and can be spotted by their droopy ears and reduced milk production. All these things can be the result of mixing several different herds together and exposing all the animals to any virus or germs that any of the groups is carrying.

As the animals parade through the parlor six by six to be relieved of their white liquid, those that appear newly ill are identified. While Daddy watches the milking machines, I jump up and balance on the curb above the pit. From this precarious perch, my goal is to insert a thermometer to obtain a rectal temperature. Those with high fevers will be diverted into our four-stanchion sickroom that lies just off the milking parlor, where they will receive further care later this morning. Animals that the vet saw in the last few days and that are already being treated can be given their antibiotic shots in the parlor. It is just necessary to stay out of the way of any kicks resulting from the sharp poke of the needle aimed at their unsuspecting leg muscles. It becomes essential, as well, to keep track of which animals have been treated so that we can keep their milk out of the milk tank. Forgetting to keep antibiotic-contaminated milk out of the milk tank can mean that we have to dump the whole tank of milk down the drain. This is an unforgiveable offense.

I feel overwhelmed at times by the responsibility of trying to be perfect and never make a mistake, by the need to keep everything straight in this confusing mess. I don't want it to be my fault if this farming venture should fail. However, the weight of blameworthiness that I see as mine feels suffocating at times.

Milking takes twice as long now, with all the illnesses. This is especially so since we are trying to combine some of the health-care needs with our regular milking routine. It is late morning by the time I head to the house for breakfast. As I walk out the milk-house door, I can hear Daddy's booming voice rise above the rattle of the bunk feeder as he shouts at Joseph.

"I don't know what's wrong with you. You're always trying to get out of work. I know you didn't scrape that one row of stalls. Go back and do it again before you come for breakfast."

It seems like Daddy is never happy with Joseph's work, no matter how he does it, so he has pretty much stopped trying. I hate the tension that is always in the air between them. I sigh at the futility of it all and keep on walking. Mostly I cope by pretending that I don't notice. Sometimes, I scream at Joseph too, because he is never on time to help me either—but then how can he be when he is always given the most difficult work and the most primitive tools to perform it. I find this to be cruel and demeaning.

I barely sit down at the table before I see the blue truck with the special doors in the back box pull up at the milk house. The veterinarian is here, and I don't want to miss helping him. I gobble a few bites, grab my coat, and head back out again. The veterinarian has become a frequent visitor at our farm, and I have developed a friendly, collegial relationship with him. I enjoy the visits, as it gives me someone from the outside to chat amicably with, and I have come to enjoy learning about the health care of the cows. In addition, Daddy allows me to call the vet when needed and to order the drugs I think we need from a mail order catalog center. This gives me a sense of control over this part of my life and contributes to my growing involvement with the cows.

Dr. Groves, a short stocky man with a crop of thinning hair, is poised beside the cow we have left in the sickroom for him. His stethoscope buds fill his ears as he listens intently through the bell to the sounds inside the triangular area formed by the ribs, the backbone, and the hip bones on the left side of the animal. He rhythmically snaps the cow's side with his thumb and index finger while he listens. I wait patiently while he completes the ritual, then acknowledge his nod of greeting.

"She has a displaced abomasum (a cow's fourth stomach)," is his verdict. "We need to open her up and tack it down where it belongs."

"How can you tell?" I ask.

He hands me his stethoscope and while I listen intently, he repeats the snapping all around her side. Mostly what I hear is a dull thudding, but then I hear a high-pitched ping, ping that sounds like someone snapping a very full balloon.

"That's it," he says. "The stomach fills with air and floats up from its normal position on the floor of the right side. This prevents the food from moving through properly."

While Dr. Groves goes out to his truck to gather the necessary supplies for the planned operation, I retrieve a hay bale to use as our instrument table. I find the prospect of an operation on a cow fascinating, and I am eager to see and assist. It is really a rather simple and crude procedure that we will perform here, in the unsterile atmosphere of a farmyard. There is no general anesthetic, and the animal must stand up so that we can do what needs to be done. A generous amount of local anesthetic is injected into the cow's left flank and then the knife turns the black hide into a widening red yawn. The veterinarian's arm disappears deep inside the cow as he fastens his suture into the bottom of the abomasum and then pushes the long strand of suture through the lower abdominal wall. I assist by holding a 2x4 against the animal's belly to provide a firm surface against which he can push. A cow's underside, unfortunately, is within easy reach of her back foot, so I need to be on the alert and ready to dodge that most popular of cow weapons. The first suture needs to be held then, while a second one is pushed through by the vet, about two inches away from the first one. Then the sutures are tied together—and the stomach is securely fastened back in its place. Participating in procedures like this energize me and help to satisfy my innate curiosity. I find it fun. While Dr. Groves meticulously stitches closed the yawning cavern, we talk about our lives specifically and farming in general.

By now it is close to noon, and there are several other sick cows that need to be seen. The vet helps me find and sort out the other animals that need our attention. Then he systematically checks temperatures, listens to their hearts and lungs, and makes a treatment plan. Some receive antibiotic shots, and some are given intravenous fluids. The noon-day sun has gone over its peak by the time he leaves. I hurriedly clean up the room and hose it down with the pressure washer before heading in for dinner.

As I walk toward the house, I glance off to the left. I can see the blue panels being bolted together on the new Harvester silo that is being erected. The Harvester will join the stave silo that stood there alone. Last week, when the temperature was forty degrees, the silo company dug the footer and poured the concrete. Now, the blue steel structure is slowly being pushed up into the sky toward its final ninety-foot height. It will provide a place to store the haylage, which is a chopped form of hay made before the hay is completely dry and with less labor required. This additional food will be needed for our growing dairy herd. Harvesters are considered to be the Cadillac of silos. The advertising pitch says that the feed will be preserved better than in a conventional silo because the atmosphere inside is free of oxygen (which causes spoilage) once the silo is filled. The only catch is that the price is also in the range of a Cadillac compared to the price of a stave or concrete silo.

As I continue toward the house, I have to remember to pick my feet up over the frozen humps and bumps of ground that snake from the machine shed to the barn. Just three weeks ago, it was discovered that the existing well could not support the needs of the dairy herd, and the pump was pumping dirt into the water tank. A new well needed to be drilled in the dead of winter—another huge unexpected expense. The local well driller, being an eighty-year-old man, was not eager to drill with the temperature at zero degrees, but he agreed to do so with Paul's help.

Once the well was dug, the next challenge was to dig in the water pipe leading from the well to the barn. In Minnesota, the ground is rock solid in January. Just digging with a backhoe is not an option. A plan was devised to lay hot coals over the ground in the planned path of the line to thaw the ground for digging. Daddy and Paul spent a week working on this before they were finally able to get the line dug to the barn.

I continue on my way to the house. I am hungry and cold and looking forward to a quiet afternoon. During our late midday meal, Daddy mentions that he is planning on having the artificial insemination (AI) company come and teach him how to breed the cows himself. Apparently they have a kind of on-the-farm education program to do that. Then we would only have to buy the semen to impregnate our cows, and we wouldn't have to always pay for the company man to come and to do it. My interest is piqued. I have become increasingly dedicated to caring for the cows, and this is a very specialized skill involved in their care—one that not everyone knows.

I interject, "I want to learn how too."

Daddy hesitates and then concedes, "Well, I guess we could both learn."

After dinner, I retire to my bedroom for a couple of hours of alone time before afternoon chores call again. At least in the winter, there are no crops to plant or cultivate or harvest. I crawl under the covers, turn on the radio for background, and pick up a book entitled *Brother Andrew*. It is one of my favorite books. It is the true story of a man who smuggles Bibles into communist countries so that the Christians there can have God's Word to read. I love the sense of risk and adventure involved in his work and the protection God gives him though it all. I want to make a difference in the world too and to have the power of God in my life, as he does in his, while bringing the good news of God's forgiveness and salvation to others. But I know that that is probably never going to happen for me. In my world, there are always cows to be milked. In fact, we rarely go anywhere other than church. In spite of wanting to read, I soon give in to my ever-present weariness and fall asleep.

Far too soon, the alarm is insisting that I arise. It is time to make my way back to the barn and perform the evening milking ritual.

Church is to be at our house today, February 16. The men of the group still have not been able to find a church to buy, so we have continued to meet in our homes. I really enjoy Sundays. The friendship with the Wiehler family has grown. Paul and Andrew, a solidly built young man with a crop of thick brown hair, spend their Sunday afternoons chatting about farming and other common interests. Joseph and Michael, a younger, thinner version of Andrew, have also built a kinship. I find friendship with all of the young people in the family. For everyone, closeness has developed through our times of laughter and sharing. The Wiehlers feel like family to all of us.

This worship service is like any other. We sing hymns together and then Peter Wiehler preaches the sermon. Clean-shaven and dressed in a plain, flat-collared suit coat with suspenders, he reminds me of the old-time saints pictured in books. But the likeness to other services changes with Peter's closing words. "I have something I need to share with you today. I sold the farm, and we will be moving to northern Minnesota in a few weeks."

Where they are moving is three hundred miles away and at the opposite end of Minnesota. We are all shocked and speechless. Peter does not offer any explanation as to why he has made this decision. But we know instantly that it means the small, struggling group of church pioneers will no longer have a minister. More importantly, the friends who have become so much a part of our lives will be gone.

Paul, at nineteen years of age, rarely cries, but this afternoon, he retreats to his room and sobs. I am just stunned. This is the last straw in our world that includes pretty much only work. Instead of families moving into the area and increasing the size of our small Mennonite group, families are now moving away. We all feel abandoned and crushed that the people we thought were our good friends have abruptly made this decision to leave, without any consultation with the rest of the group. Daddy and Mama, along with Paul, decide to make a visit to Peter and Brenda's home tomorrow to try to talk them out of moving. I know that they are not going to change their minds, so I do not see any point in making the effort and do not accompany them. Everything about this move to Minnesota is starting to feel like a mistake and beyond my ability to influence its outcome.

The cold, frozen days of January and February have given way to the season of mud. March and April in Minnesota are defined by the depth of that mud. My personal life has become a repetition of milking, caring for sick cows, introducing new calves to the world, recording all that—and then breeding the cows again so that there will be a new crop of calves in nine months.

My day begins, as does every day, with jumping out of bed when the alarm goes off at the new, earlier time of 4:00 a.m. I force my body to go through the motions of dressing before braving the elements during my walk to the barn in the shadow of the yard light. At least it is not as cold now. A hint of spring is in the air. If I have any doubts about that, my feet slip this way and that in the thick goo that is the base of every walking and driving surface around the farm.

I flip on the light switches in the milk house and then the parlor as I make my way through to the sick-cow area. My first order of business is to check on the cow that we left in the calving pen for the night. The ligaments at the top of a bovine's pelvic area relax about twelve to twenty-four hours before she will give birth. I am ever-vigilant, watching for this telltale sign on the non-milking pregnant cows that are getting close to delivery. Seeing that relaxation last evening on this particular heifer, I decided to place her in the pen. That way, she could have her baby here in the clean, dry straw, rather than in the cold, wet, manure that covers the floor of the main free-stall barn. I had also stumbled out of my warm bed at 2:00 a.m. to check on her. But there was no sign of any calf yet. Now, I find a new calf being vigorously licked by its excited mother. She encourages her baby with a series of short moos and head butts. The sooner the calf can be fed, the better the chance that it will not become ill with scours (diarrhea) or any other of the myriad diseases that seem to lurk on this farm. I retrieve a bucket and call on my hand-milking skills. I need to extract just enough colostrum, or first milk, to make sure this new little one gets about two quarts of its mother's milk. Modern dairy calves do not seem to have the instinct any longer to just get up and drink from one of the available spigots. That is why this exercise is so important. This calf is cooperative and drinks readily from the bottle nipple I offer him, which is a relief. Some are not so agreeable, and then it is a frustrating battle to get that precious first liquid into their tummies.

Because I took care of the new calf first, we are late getting started with the milking. My eyes want to drift shut as I wait for some milking machines to finish their task. The milking this morning goes reasonably well, meaning that there is only one fresh cow to add to the milking lineup and only one other recently fresh animal that seems to be off her feed. I place her in the sickroom for the veterinarian to look at later. Every day presents far more sick cows than there should be. Just a few weeks ago, Daddy finally had the vet come and take some blood samples from the sicker cows to send for analysis. This was so we could try to determine just what the main problem is. We still haven't gotten any definite answers.

After breakfast, my first order of business is to climb onto the top of the free-stall front. From here, I have a good view of all the cows. I stand quietly and scan the herd for about thirty minutes. I am watching for any cows that are being mounted and standing still for their buddies. "Riding" the "in heat" animal by others in the herd is the sign that she would be most friendly to a bull—if one were anywhere near. But since we don't use a bull, it is up to me to figure out when those cows that have been milking for a couple of months are ovulating, so that they can be artificially inseminated.

It has only been about six weeks since the American Breeders representative came to begin educating Daddy and me in the skill of artificial insemination. We started out watching slides of the bovine reproductive tract. Then we proceeded to practicing on a preserved set of genuine cow parts. The process seemed pretty simple. A couple of weeks later, the breeder came back and reviewed all the information for a second time. Then it was time to try it on a real cow. That was a whole different experience. To actually inseminate a cow, one needs to put on a long plastic glove and insert one's arm into the rectum of the cow. With the other hand, a pipette containing the semen is inserted into the vagina. The trick then is to use the gloved hand to manipulate the pipette through the rings of the cervix and deposit the thawed semen just inside the uterus. To me, it seems a little like a blind man feeling around in a dark, slippery hole for an earthworm and then trying to feed it with the other hand. I am kind of getting the hang of it after several weeks of practice. I am proud of my new skill and the contribution it will make to the success of our farming venture. My biggest desire is to be one of the "boys," and this moves me a step closer, in my eyes, to that coveted role. Somehow, I have picked up the sense that the contributions of the menfolk are more valued than those of Mama, who just takes care of the household tasks. I have come to believe that housekeeping and gardening are looked down on by Daddy, as they provide no visible revenue. Yes, Mama still works as a nurse and her job provides the revenue to keep us fed and clothed. But she is left to struggle alone most of the time with the cleaning, cooking, washing, and baking as the laboring hands are needed for the "real" work of farming.

My vigil on top of the world is interrupted by the arrival of the veterinarian.

"Good morning," I say.

He nods and then gets down to business. After carefully listening with his stethoscope, he diagnoses another displaced abomasum or, as we have come to call it, a "twisted stomach." He begins the now-familiar surgery to correct it. But today, after making the incision and inserting his arm, his eyebrows scrunch together.

"I don't understand it, but I don't find anything wrong."

He feels around carefully for any other obvious problem, such as hardware disease, in which a cow might have swallowed a nail or other sharp object while eating, but he finds nothing. Dr. Groves carefully stitches the opening closed and treats the cow with intravenous fluids, antibiotics, and a magnet. The magnet is shoved down the cow's throat with a long "pill gun" in the hopes that it will stay in her stomach and attract the irritating object if that is what is causing the loss of appetite.

He shrugs and says, "I don't know what is wrong with her. The only choice is to treat her symptomatically and hope that she gets better."

I get a sinking feeling in my stomach. *How am I going to tell Daddy about this?* Our veterinarian bill has become a significant source of stress between Daddy and me, as I find myself needing to call the vet several times a week for sick animals.

I need to hurry and change clothes once the vet has left if I am going to make it to the bookmobile. I have discovered that it comes once a week for a couple of hours to the little town hall building that is just a couple of miles from our place. Books and reading are my recreation in this world of work, and I don't want to miss my opportunity. Reading is the activity that saves me from insanity and total hopelessness. I can lose myself in someone else's adventure for a few hours and then spend many more hours creating my own imaginary life based on the books. By eleven, I am home with two books, *Hot Rod* and *High School Dropout*. I carefully lay them on my bedside table for later enjoyment.

I return to the barn to wash out the sickroom stanchion area and to clean up the calving pen for the next cow. I retrieve those most handy tools, the wheelbarrow and fork, and load the now-soiled straw from the pen into the wheelbarrow. I will dump my cargo outside for Paul to later load onto the big, automated manure spreader. Then I wash out the room. The water being pumped through the hose at high pressure propels the manure—and everything else in its path—out the door into the pit. Ah, this works like a charm. I hang onto the hose with a firm grip. I once dropped the hose while the pump was running, and it became a squirming, violently lashing snake from which retreat was the only safe response.

I am just hanging up the hose when Daddy comes by.

"What did the veterinary find on that cow?"

I suck in my breath and hesitate before replying. "He thought she had a twisted stomach so he opened her up, but he couldn't find anything." I stop and search Daddy's face.

Angry lines form on his forehead, and his bushy rimmed eyes bore into me until I look away. "He's just doing this on purpose to try to get as much money out of us as possible." A dark color creeps up his neck and into his face. His voice rises. "I can't afford to pay for his mistakes anymore. We need to find a different veterinary."

I don't want to find a different veterinarian. I consider Dr. Groves to be my friend, and I look forward to his visits. "He made a mistake, but he's doing the best he can. It's not his fault we have so many sick cows." I speak to the floor.

Instantly, Daddy's arms stiffen at his sides, and his voice escalates into an irate growl. "You're far too friendly with him. I'm beginning to think there is more to your relationship with him than taking care of cows, and I won't have it."

I catch the implication of his words, and I feel like I have been slapped. I did not see that coming. I stare at him as he turns and storms away.

I make my way into the office with the intent of gathering the things I will need to take care of recording the new-calf information after dinner. But my eyes blur with the tears I feel coming, making it impossible to focus. I feel misunderstood and wrongly accused. I am crushed, and I allow myself to be overcome by sobs. I can't believe that this is my life. I try so hard to do the right thing, and this is what I get. I can't stop the crying, but I know there will be no discussion and no apologies, so I might as well keep dragging myself through my now-spoiled day. I have no desire to go to the house for dinner, so I dig out the camera, a new ear tag, and the bottle of calf dehorner. I methodically go through the motions of my waiting tasks.

Later, I slip into my bedroom. Reading my books has no appeal right now either, so I escape into an intermittent sleep for the rest of the afternoon.

I can hear the rumble of the four-wheel-drive tractor as Paul pulls the new seven-bottom plow through the soil that didn't get plowed last fall. The trees and flowers have erupted into full bloom. Hope is renewed; this year, we will be prepared to plant when the sun shines.

It is a warm May morning. I breed two cows after breakfast, take some stitches out of another cow that has had surgery, and spend some time arranging drugs on the shelves of a cabinet Daddy has bought for storage in the utility room. Mama, her long, braided brown hair sticking out in all directions, is napping on the couch after a night shift at the hospital, but she wants my help with doing the wash after she wakes up. Therefore, I only spend a couple of hours in the barn.

As I walk back to the house, I notice a pickup parked by the silos. Today, the two-way radio system that Daddy bought is being installed. There will be an antenna on the silos, with a base station in the office just off of the milk house. Each enclosed tractor, the combine, the Uni, and the pickup will all have a radio unit, as well as the house. This means we can get in touch whenever we need to, whether to call everyone to dinner or to call for more seed corn or fertilizer. Daddy thinks that being able to stay in touch will save time and money that would otherwise be wasted in running around over our two sections of land.

Mama opens the puffy eyes embedded in her little round face as I slam the kitchen door, and she mumbles, "I must get up."

I wait patiently while she puts her glasses and head covering back on. Then she and I make our way to the basement. Mama only washes once a week, on Mondays, as we still have a wringer washer. All the clothes must be agitated by hand in one end of the big washer tub and then run through the wringer into the equally big rinse tub. Once each piece of clothing is dipped up and down for rinsing, it then must be guided again through the wringer into the waiting wash basket. I emerge from the dark cool basement with the wet clothes and hang them on the line to dry. I can soak in the sunshine and listen to the noises of the farm while I work.

The backhoe, with Joseph's trim figure positioned at the wheel, spins down the driveway, headed for the field to pick up rocks. Large rocks seem to make their way to the surface of the land each year, and if left there, they can cause breakdowns when they get picked up or are run into by the equipment. Picking up rocks is a necessary but back-breaking chore. Joseph gets assigned

this yearly task while Paul and Daddy go about the more important tasks of running the farm—at least that is my impression.

I hear another crunch of tires on the driveway, and I turn to
see who else is here. A tall, hefty, and handsome gentleman gets
out of the pickup. I smile. Andrew Wiehler has arrived. He is
coming to stay with us for several weeks to help with the planting. Daddy and Mama were unable to convince his father, Peter,
to stay in the area, but the bond between Paul and Andrew has
continued to thrive. We are all thrilled that Andrew is staying
for the time being.

As we convene around the dinner table, the conversation is
relaxed and pleasant. Having Andrew here will be good. It will
provide a barrier to Daddy's common practice of criticizing Joseph
at mealtimes for all his real and perceived failings.

"I am going to town for a load of shavings this afternoon,"
Daddy mentions during the course of the dinner conversation.
The wood shavings will be used to put some bedding on the mats
in the hope that the cows will stay drier. The mats are designed
to be used without bedding, but we have discovered that the mats
are often damp. Daddy is hoping that adding some shavings will
keep the cows cleaner and that fewer of them will have mastitis,
an infection of the udder. I hope so too.

"Can I go along too?" I ask, excited about the possibility of a
trip off of the farm.

"Yes."

I enjoy the ride away from the farm, but by the time we get
home, it is time for milking. Paul is still working in the field,
and Daddy is busy unloading the shavings. I start milking alone.
I hate milking alone. It is exhausting to have to do everything
myself, and it takes me twice as long. Joseph is supposed to come
and help when he is done feeding the heifers, but Joseph sees no
need to hurry to get on to the next boring job, regardless of who

is screaming at him to do so. When Joseph finally comes to help, I rant and rave at him. "Why do you always have to be late? You're supposed to be done with the heifers before it's time to milk." He just shrugs and does not respond.

I eventually calm down, and some of my feeling of "nobody cares" resolves—at least temporarily. In spite of my irritation with Joseph at times, he is still my confidante on this farm, and we often share our disappointments and commiserate. In a little bit, Joseph shares with me, "I climbed up to the top of the little silo today and walked around on the top."

I am horrified. The silo is forty feet tall and is almost empty now. It has no roof, just an endless expanse of sky above it. Walking around the top on the six-inch ledge has to be a lot like walking a tightrope—but with nothing to grab onto if one should fall.

"You're going to fall off and kill yourself," I scold.

He just laughs. I have always known my younger brother has a propensity for daring adventure.

"Don't you have any sense at all?" he has been scolded by Daddy more than once for riding heifers like he is in the rodeo, but I suspect he still does it when no one is looking.

It is eight thirty in the evening before the chores are finally wrapped up and nine before we sit down for supper. Then it is off to bed by ten thirty. Such a late supper will become the routine during the busy planting season, for here in Minnesota, the sun does not sink below the horizon before nine o'clock in the evening. And there is much work to be done while the sun shines.

It is the beginning of June, and about two thirds of the corn, or five hundred fifty acres, is planted. Out of our twelve hundred eighty acres, only about eight hundred to nine hundred acres are currently tillable. The other three hundred to four hundred acres are a huge swamp or wetland. During the wet, rainy spring, a couple of ponds graced the area. Also, on the north end of the farm, there are still a couple hundred acres of last year's corn that need to be harvested. This project will be saved for last and that land will then be planted into soybeans. We have an additional hundred acres that will also be planted into corn, but we need to take a break from planting to empty the manure pit. It will be the last opportunity to spread the manure on the fields until after the crops are harvested in the fall.

The roar of the tractor with the throttle wide open fills my ears, and the stench overwhelms my nostrils. It is not an understatement to say that the "whole world stinks." Some people affectionately call this "country-fresh air." Today, Paul is agitating the manure in the pit under the barn into slurry so that it can be pumped into liquid manure tanks and hauled to the field. The new manure pump arrived just a couple of days ago.

This is the first time since we put cows into the new barn that the pit will be emptied. The pit is about ten feet deep, and it lies under the whole length and width of the free-stall barn. It can hold about six months' worth of manure and parlor runoff. To allow access so that the liquid manure can be agitated and pumped, there are six evenly spaced openings in the slatted concrete floor of the barn. These are normally covered with metal plates. There is always a concern that cows can fall into the pit if diligent care is not exercised to keep the cows away from whatever opening is uncovered while pumping. This is something we do not want to happen. Adequate ventilation of the building has also been stressed to us as a priority. Allowing the methane gas that is stirred up to build up to a high concentration can cause the deaths of people and livestock. This whole operation sounds rather risky to me, but I am still fascinated and want to see what is going on.

While Paul is running the agitator pump, Andrew has been getting the "honey wagons" ready for hauling. We own only one liquid manure hauling tank, so Daddy went to a little town just ten miles north of us to bring home one he has borrowed from a farmer there. Just a few weeks ago, someone mentioned to Daddy that a farmer close by had an operation similar to ours. Daddy went off to see if he could make an agreement whereby the two of them could trade off equipment. Since pumping is only necessary twice a year, it allows both parties to have the use of more equipment without the additional capital outlay.

While the "boys" work on emptying the manure pit, I go about my work of taking some pictures of the heifer calves that were born in the last week. I have only three calves to do today. Each one will have a numbered ear tag pushed through its ear and then, since most of them will lose the tags before they become cows, I take photographs. I push and pull the first calf out into the sunshine and place it against the backdrop of the silo. I spend several minutes trying to position its feet so that I can see all four legs in the picture. Of course, as soon as I step back to snap the picture, a least one leg has moved or the calf is looking somewhere other than at me. The calf and I go through this dance numerous times until I am finally fast enough to outwit my uncooperative partner. I am using a Kodak black-and-white instant camera, so the pictures develop before my eyes, and I can immediately proceed to pasting them in a thickening photo album. Under each set of pictures will be the date of the animal's birth and the names of the mother (or dam) and the father (or sire). This will be used primarily for informational purposes when the little calves become milking cows in about two to three years.

After dinner, Daddy is visited by a tiling contractor that he has contacted. One of Daddy's goals this second year is to make the three hundred to four hundred acres of wet, untillable land into productive farm land. This will require "tiling" it. During the process of tiling, four-inch corrugated plastic tubing, with slits throughout, is pulled about three feet underground with a special machine. The tubing is buried in a grid pattern across the field and then attached together, with an outlet into a ditch. This allows the water that was previously trapped in a marsh or pond to drain away, and presto, the land can be farmed. I listen for several hours while Daddy outlines what he would like to do, while at the same time saying over and over that we don't have any money to do this.

A couple of weeks pass. The manure is all hauled, and all six hundred fifty acres of corn are planted. Next comes the task of harvesting the two hundred acres of corn on the north half section that was too wet for harvest last fall. It is late June, and the weather has turned hot and sticky. Daddy started out a couple of days ago trying to combine the corn. He soon realized that the corn was nothing more than miniature cornflakes. He switched over to chopping as much of it for silage as possible.

On Independence Day, we finish planting our two hundred acres of soybeans. It took about two weeks to harvest the last corn, work the ground, and replant the field. In Minnesota, the saying is that the corn must be "knee high by the fourth of July" if the crop is to mature before the frost. Most of our corn has made that hallmark this year—all except for the last one hundred acres, which can be used for silage if need be. I haven't heard any such saying about soybeans, but we are pretty much the last ones in the community planting beans so, we hope that this year does not turn out to be a repeat of last year's fiasco. That would definitely put an end to this farming venture.

Since the Wiehler family moved in May as planned, Sunday has become a day without a plan due, I think, to a certain despondency that has settled over everyone. Since Andrew has now left also, a change is evident in Paul's demeanor. He talks little and mostly works by himself out in the shed. Andrew stayed with us through the end of June and then went north to be with his family. The remaining families in the fellowship group have slowly disbanded since the loss of their minister and the development of some conflicts between the various members. Consequently, we rarely go anywhere, with the occasional exception of a visit to another group that has been putting down roots about thirty-five miles northwest of our place. This will become the pattern for our religious practice over the next two years.

A typical Sunday begins, of course, with milking the cows. The nice part is that I can usually depend on having help on this day. After breakfast, Daddy has us gather together at the table and go over the Sunday-school lesson from our Mennonite publishing house study books, or "quarterlies," as they are called. Paul, Joseph, and I have become more reluctant to have any kind of Bible study together as a family, due to the growing tension between Daddy and us. Differences of opinion are not encouraged, so our study is more of a dissertation by Daddy on his version of what is right in the world. And to Daddy, everything that is different from the way he sees it has to be sinful. So there is mostly silence when questions are presented for discussion, and our lesson does not take long to complete.

I spend the rest of my Sunday morning in my room listening

to the radio and to Mennonite a cappella music on audio tapes while I read. I have found that music soothes my soul and provides comfort to my troubled heart. I have sneaked the "funnies" (cartoon section) from the newspaper into my room to read in private. Reading the newspaper on Sunday is a "sin" in and of itself, but reading the cartoons is forbidden on any day. I simply find them entertaining, and I am starting to brush aside my father's assertions by telling myself that *what Daddy doesn't know won't hurt him.*

When I finish with the newspaper, I pick up where I left off in my reading of the book *All Creatures Great and Small.* Books are my best friends. This story presents the everyday life and struggles of a Scottish veterinarian. I find myself laughing out loud at his escapades. I have had a growing interest in the veterinarian aspect of my herdsman job and find myself pulled in this direction. Not only have I been reading veterinarian stories, I have also been spending numerous hours reading about animal diseases and their treatments. I have even secretly sent off a request for information about a veterinarian assistant program that looks interesting. I read until my eyelids slide down over my corneas, and I just can't prevent them from closing any longer. I sleep for several hours, until I am called for lunch.

In the afternoon, I decide to venture out into the sunshine. The sunshine always lifts my spirits, as does the invigorating activity of a bicycle ride. I pedal west down the gravel road for two miles, make a left turn and pedal for another mile, then turn east for another two miles. Finally, I ride north the mile back to the farm. This has become my bike riding loop. It takes me away from the farm at least for a short distance. I can feel the wind in my face and be free of work for a few minutes. In our part of Minnesota, determining a riding path is a simple proposition as the roads are laid out in mile squares. Getting lost is never a problem.

By the time I return, it is time for milking. I resent that Daddy sees Sunday afternoons as his time off and often doesn't show up to help milk until later. I don't get any days when I can have someone else do my work, so I begrudge him that luxury. But if I am lucky, Paul will help, and we will get done a little earlier tonight than we do during the week. Though we don't talk a lot, Paul and I get along well together. Tonight, he sits on the step leading into the parlor and ruminates about the future.

"Someday, I am going to get married and have some children to bounce on my knee." He says.

I chuckle at his dreams. "How are you going to do that without any women to marry?"

"I don't know," he says. "I'll figure it out somehow."

Paul loves to play ball, and if we have time after milking, he will persuade Joseph and me to spend some time playing baseball, pitch and catch, horseshoes, or some other such thing. Our laughter blends together, and we put away the work for a few minutes.

Our troubles with sick cows have not improved. Dr. Groves comes at least a couple of times every week. There are "twisted stomachs," high fevers, and mastitis to treat, and cows that just plain won't eat that need to be looked at. A few of the cows look like walking skeletons, and, one by one, they finally become so weak that they can't get up by themselves. It has become a regular occurrence for either Joseph or I, and sometimes both of us, to need to push a cow out of the free stall that she has become stuck in. We prop our backs against the front of the free stall, place our feet on the cow's shoulder, then push with all we have in us until the animal slides out onto the slatted floor. Once on the floor, she can usually gain enough momentum to get up at least one more time. I just hate doing this. Not only is it hard, fruitless work, but seeing the cows like this is discouraging. I just wish we could figure out what is wrong.

Daddy has not mentioned his accusations regarding the vet to me again, but I tread carefully when discussing anything regarding him. Daddy complains regularly that "he doesn't know what he is doing" and that "he charges way too much," but with the exception of calling another veterinarian from a different town a few times, he still allows me to call Dr. Groves. I feel my stomach curl into a knot, though, every time we are discussing anything to do with the health care of the cows. I can never be sure what words are going to come out of his mouth. I often feel like I am just not what he expects me to be and that this state of affairs is somehow my fault.

A couple of weeks ago, a veterinarian from the University of Minnesota, along with two students, came to spend the day on the farm. They asked all kinds of questions and took numerous blood samples in an effort to find out why we are still having so many problems with "failure to thrive" cows. The current thinking is that the corn silage from last fall might be high in nitrates and of poor quality because of its undeveloped state at harvest.

In spite of the reason that they were on our farm, I enjoyed the day. I loved working with the "experts" and helping to try to solve the mystery. One day, soon after that visit, Dr. Groves turns to me as he is getting ready to give a cow some intravenous medicine.

"Would you like to try inserting the needle?"

My face brightens, and I nod. "Sure."

Not only is it a skill I would love to learn, but if I could give the IV medications, I could treat a lot of the cows myself, and the veterinarian wouldn't need to come as often. That would save us a significant amount of money, and Daddy should be pleased with that.

Giving an intravenous medication to a cow is a tricky process, but once learned, it is one that I can and will repeat hundreds of times over the next ten years. I consider myself physically strong, and I am not afraid to tackle any job that a man can do. In fact, in high school, I prided myself on being able to beat any boy at arm wrestling. I take the "nose leader," a sort of pliers-like device with two ball-shaped devices on the end that opens, and attempt to slip it into the cow's nose. But maybe "slip" is not the appropriate term; I wrestle to get a grip on the cow's mouth. The trick is to pin the moving head against the stanchions and then make a dive for the nose holes with the nose leader. Once the nose has been captured, it is simply a matter of applying brute strength to pull the large head to one side and secure it to a stanchion pipe using the nostril grabber.

Now the fun part begins. The jugular vein lies in the groove that runs parallel with the contour of the neck. I place my left hand into the groove to constrict the blood return from the head. This causes the vein to bulge into a finger-sized garden hose under the skin. The right hand is used to plunge the needle into the vein in a quick, purposeful motion. Success is signaled by a stream of dark red blood spewing forth. The hard part is done at this point. It is simply a matter of attaching the tubing and watching the life-restoring fluid flow in. I have watched the vet many times. It all looks so simple, but my first attempt does not go quite that well. The bulge slips off to the side, and I end up poking everything but vein. Then, of course, the cow does not understand that I am trying to help her, and she keeps throwing her head around every time she feels that sharp poke. With the guidance of Dr. Grove's expert hands, we do finally get the job done. And now I feel empowered to try it on my own. I am proud of my new accomplishment.

The trees are turning color and beginning to drop their leaves. The roar of the Field Queen in the distance, followed by the intermittent whirl and clunk of the silage as it makes it journey up the pipe and into the silo, fills the air each day. Daddy and Paul have been busy filling silo. Joseph and I are assigned the task of driving over the field with the backhoe after it has been chopped and picking up the ears of corn that have been knocked onto the ground by the advancing chopper.

"Why do we have to pick up corn by hand?" I ask. "No one else does this."

"We can't waste any of our crop," Daddy insists.

It is very tiring jumping off the tractor over and over again and stooping to hand pick ears of corn off the ground. I am glad when that task, which I consider to be unnecessary, is finished. Daddy and Paul pause for a week from the chopping to empty the manure pit a second time onto the newly cleared ground. Hopefully, the pit will not need to be emptied again until next spring.

I spend my morning after milking today reading the local newspaper and the *Budget* (Ohio), an Amish-Mennonite newspaper. The *Budget* is a compilation of letters from "scribes," or writers, in various communities all over the country, telling of the happenings in the lives of other Amish and Mennonite families. The letters hold a certain fascination to me as, it seems, all kinds of strange and exciting things happen in other people's lives. In contrast, my life is the same stressful combination of work and sleep and nothingness every day. I have started to become increasingly more discouraged and just plain tired of the life that is mine. Daddy's response to any voicing of this weariness is, "God gave us all these gifts. We need to be good stewards and work hard to take care of them."

After about an hour of reading, I make my way to the barn to stand upon my perch, from which I scout for cows that I will need to breed later in the day. Then it is time to hook the gooseneck cattle trailer to the pickup and take the bull calves that have been born in the last week to the sale barn. It is a job I enjoy. It does take a special skill to back a gooseneck trailer around, and I am proud that I have mastered it. Not many women can do what I do on a daily basis.

As I return from my fifty-mile round trip, I notice a car in front of the house. Daddy is talking to a building salesman. I step inside in time to see him signing a contract for another machine shed. My heart drops. *Just what we need. More buildings to pay for.* I am feeling depressed, but the day is warm, so I walk out into the pasture to check on the dry cows. I lie on the grass in the pasture, with the sun on my face, and allow the tears to course down my cheeks and onto the fading grass of summer. *Oh God! Help us!* is all that I can pray. I want my life to be about more than paying for buildings and cows.

October is birthday month at our house. Joseph turns seventeen years old on October 9. Then, I turn eighteen on October 14, followed by Paul becoming twenty on October 26. Mama makes a special meal for us on our respective birthdays, but beyond that, birthdays are just another day of work in our lives. The beginning of combining of the corn is the important event that occurs on Joseph's special day, and the crop this year looks promising. The good crop leads to another sort of problem though: Where are we going to put all the corn? There is only one small bin and the flat-roofed machine shed currently on the farm to store the corn in. Daddy decides to order a fifteen-thousand-bushel grain bin to be built yet this fall. In the meantime, the harvesting begins.

The air is cool and crisp, but the sun feels warm through the window of the truck. I shift through the gears until I get up to highway cruising speed. Our small grain bin is full, and the shed is filling rapidly. The only option now is to haul the corn to the town elevator for storage. Between milkings, this has become my job. It is an eight-mile trip to town, best used for thinking and listening to the radio. The bins at the elevator reflect the sunlight onto the line of various-sized trucks and tractors with grain wagons, waiting to unload. Throughout the morning, the line has been steadily lengthening, and by mid-morning, it requires an hour and a half to two hours of idleness before one can unload. All I can do is wait patiently until it is my turn to drive into the dumping area. I step into the weigh building, where the operator checks the flashing numbers on the scale display, and then it is back to the truck to raise the bed. The corn comes cascading off in a cloud of dust into the hungry auger and, within ten minutes, I am on my way back for another load.

The combining has been put on hold while we put up the new bin. Daddy went to South Dakota with the semi two days ago to pick up the disassembled bin. Today, everyone is expected to put their hands to the task of assembling the bin. The foundation was poured about a week ago, and it is ready for us. Paul and I drag two sheets of shiny, curved metal onto the concrete. A caulking material needs to be put between the overlapping edges of the sheets and then a "million" bolts need to be ratcheted into the predrilled holes. This is not a hard task, but it is tedious and time-consuming. More sheets are added to the ring until it comes together in a completed circle. Next, the roof is assembled and attached. Then it is time to add the jacks that will be used to lift the top ring and roof so that another ring can be added underneath it. Once another ring is completed, flat metal bars are added to the outside as stiffeners. This process will be repeated over and over again until seven rings have been lifted into the air and the bin stands ready to receive its load of yellow gold. My fingers cramp and stiffen. It is the last day of October, and the temperature is in the forties. It is a good thing that I decided to put long corduroy pants on under my dress. Even so, my knees creak and protest at being exposed over and over again to the cold concrete. Keeping the body moving is the only way to stay warm. I am more than ready to milk tonight, even if it means milking alone. At least, it will be warm in the parlor.

It is time to make the trip back East that we have been waiting for. The farm in Pennsylvania has finally sold. The selling price was only about half of what Daddy was hoping for, but it is the only serious offer Daddy has received in the last two years.

It is nine thirty on Thursday evening, December 12, before the cows are milked one last time and the suitcases loaded into the waiting car. Daddy gives his final instructions to Paul and Joseph, who are staying behind to take care of the dairy. I am thrilled to be allowed to make this trip and am looking forward to seeing friends and relatives. The backseat is all mine, and I curl up on it. Daddy drives all through the night and into the next day. The rain pelting on the windshield and the swish of the wipers invades my consciousness as I drift in and out of sleep. We arrive at the home of Nickolas Lichti around six o'clock the next evening. This family is part of the Mennonite church group that we had belonged to while living in Pennsylvania. I am excited to see Sarah, their daughter who is my age, and we chat well into the night.

Opening my eyes on Saturday morning is a struggle, but smells of baking bread reach my nostrils. The day is calling. We drive by the farm on our way to Grammy and Grandpop's, in the Philadelphia area of eastern Pennsylvania. "Reimer Road" reads the sign that stands by the deserted weathered barn. A certain longing passes over me as I stare at the remaining tribute to our past. The house stares forlornly out at us. The barn is empty; the windows are now broken. I look back one last time as Daddy drives away. There are many times that I wish we could go back.

"Are we ever going to get there?" I used to ask when we drove to Grammy's on Christmas mornings many years ago. Today, I wonder that same thing. It is only about one hundred miles from "the farm" to Grandpop's, but the traffic is bumper to bumper most of the way. In Minnesota, folks give directions to each other using estimates of how many miles to a certain place it is. After all, one can expect to drive sixty miles per hour there. In Pennsylvania's eastern section, however, folks tell the listener how much time it takes to get there, because one can never drive the speed limit. There is no choice but to go with the flow. There are not even any country roads where it might be possible to pass, as one town flows into another without any interruption.

Grammy and Grandpop meet us at the door with big hugs. They have arranged the Christmas get-together of Mama's ten remaining brothers and sisters and their families for this weekend. The laughter, sharing, and the food bring back memories of all the Christmases of my childhood. And of course, Grammy serves us homemade scrapple with apple butter for breakfast on Monday morning before we head out. Scrapple is a traditional Pennsylvania Dutch meat made from the scraps of the hog during butchering. It is one food that does not seem to be sold in Minnesota stores, and I love it.

With gifts of love stored away in the car trunk and happy

memories of our time together, we drive back to the biggest city that is close to the farm. We wait in the car at the Federal Land Bank office until our appointment at one in the afternoon. I read my book and watch the rain drops slide down the window while Daddy and Mama talk. The bank thermometer reads sixty degrees. I think about what a difference the temperature is here in Pennsylvania in December compared to in Minnesota. By closing time, the papers are signed, and we begin our journey back home.

The next day, as we start out, Daddy's leg is swollen, and Mama is worried that he has a blood clot, but he still insists on driving. He wants to get home as fast as possible. Ever the nurse, Mama gives him several aspirin to thin his blood. A couple of hours into the day, the car begins to buck intermittently. Then, to top it off, Daddy notices that there is a slow leak in one of the tires. A trip to a garage to have the tire fixed is necessary. I am tense, and my stomach muscles become tighter as the day wears on. A stabbing pain develops in the pit of my stomach, and I start to shake. I cannot make myself stop, and by the time we arrive home at eleven thirty that evening, I am shaking violently and throwing up. I recognize this as the result of the rising tension in my life that I feel helpless to control. It is not the first time this has happened, and I have no idea how to deal with it.

Under Mama's care and attention, Daddy's leg gets better over the next two weeks, but our financial situation continues to deteriorate. At the insistence of our farm lending agency, Daddy signs a contract with a real estate agent to sell the farm in Minnesota. In spite of selling the farm in Pennsylvania, he has not been able to come up with enough money to make the payments on the farm or the operating loan.

Chapter 5

The Downward Spiral

With the exception of potential buyers coming by every once in a while to look at the farm, my life after our return from Pennsylvania returns to one of milking and caring for the cattle. A box of prescription drugs, supplies, and vaccines that I had ordered to use in treating the ever present health concerns of our animals arrived yesterday. I have stashed it in the corner of the mudroom until I can find the time to tackle the job of storing the items away. This morning, Daddy noticed the conspicuous package perched on the freezer on his way in for breakfast.

"Why are you buying more drugs?" he demanded. "You are spending way too much on drugs. You can't just keep on ordering whatever you want. After this, I need to see the orders before you send them."

I do not respond but I am angry and hurt. This is a new development. Up until now, Daddy has trusted me enough to allow me to order whatever was necessary to treat the animals. I feel that I have always been responsible with what I buy, so I resent his taking away one more freedom.

I finish breakfast, pick up the box, and head out to the barn. It is a day in late February. The sun feels warm on my face but does little to warm my heart. I just wish I could disappear from this place, but there is no chance of that happening. My first task is to put away the contents of the box before Daddy actually sees them. I have bought several extra bottles of antibiotics, IV calcium, and extra boxes of mastitis treatment medicine because it is cheaper to buy in quantities. After being scolded, I am sure I would get another lecture if he actually saw how much of everything I have bought. To spare myself another tongue-lashing, I hide the extra amounts high on the shelf in the utility room behind other boxes.

Two cows are waiting in the sickroom to be bred. I scan the list of bulls for which we carry semen and choose which ones I will use. Semen is kept frozen in a tank containing liquid nitrogen. Liquid nitrogen is extremely cold at -320 degrees F. The liquid boils and steams into a fog when it comes into contact with the warmer air of the environment. I pull the holding rack out and snap the ampule I have chosen off with my bare fingers. I drop it into a warm bath to thaw. White spots of frostbite on my fingers remind me that I am supposed to do this with gloves on. After the appropriate thawing time has passed, I draw the precious liquid into a pipette and then proceed to deposit it inside the waiting cow. Hopefully, there will be a baby calf in nine months as a result.

Having completed my task, I wash out the room. I return to the office to take inventory of the semen we have. Then I need to decide which bulls' semen I will order the next time the American Breeders salesman comes around. He should be coming in the next week. At least I am still allowed to make this choice. I really don't feel much like doing anything else today in the barn, so I make my way back to the house.

Mama, her hands covered with flour, is baking the weekly shoofly pies, cakes, and other pies for our desserts that we love.

"Will you frost the cake for me?"

I dig out the powdered sugar, butter, vanilla, and milk and soon whip up a batch of vanilla frosting. The reward for me from this task is that I get to enjoy a fair sampling of the cake crumbs and frosting. I am soon finished, and I curl up in the chair in the family room to read. I pore over the information that I have received about the veterinarian assistant program. I would love to do this, but there is no use in even thinking about it. I told Daddy a few weeks ago that I wanted to be a vet, and he just frowned.

"You can use your skills here. You don't need to go to school to take care of the cows."

I sigh and reach for a book. *All Things Bright and Beautiful* seems like the perfect book to cheer me up. It is the second book in a series chronicling the humorous adventures of the British veterinarian James Herriot.

An insistent "Woff! Woff! Woff!" reaches my ears, and I glance outside. A county deputy sheriff steps out of his car and heads for the house. My heart threatens to thump right out of my chest. I wonder what he wants.

"I have a summons for Jay Reimer," he states when I open the door to his knock. I direct him to the shed where Paul and Daddy are working on the equipment. Daddy soon comes to the house with the papers. His face is expressionless, but his jaw is clenched. The papers declare the intent of the former owner to foreclose on the farm. We have known for some time that the lack of money is threatening the farm, but this is the first legal evidence. The operating loan agency has not been paid either, but Daddy has had numerous discussions with them in an attempt to renegotiate the loan and forestall any legal action. In the meantime, he has also contacted various insurance companies, hoping to obtain a loan big enough to pay everyone else off before legal action is taken.

Today is cloudy and cool. It is March; the season of mud has returned. I make my way to the barn after breakfast. The vet is scheduled to come this morning to treat another displaced abomasum. He diagnosed it last evening while he was here on an emergency call.

I made the call after watching one of the pregnant cows labor all day with nothing happening. Becoming increasingly concerned, I had finally inserted my arm into her in an effort to figure out what the problem was. The cervix did not seem to be dilated more than enough to just get my hand through. Something wasn't right, but I had no clue as to what. Dr. Groves soon arrived, and he instantly had a name for the problem: a uterine torsion. This is when, for some unknown reason, a cow's uterus turns with the unborn calf. The turn causes the cervix to twist. The only way for the calf to be delivered is to get the uterus, along with its fifty- to seventy-five-pound load of calf, to turn back the other way. Dr. Groves instructed me to bump up against the side of the cow with my knee as hard as I could while he applied a twisting leverage on the calf's feet from inside the cow. I bumped and bumped and bumped and then I switched legs and bumped some more. My thigh muscles were screaming before the whole works finally rolled over and the twist was removed. Finally, after some tugging and pulling, a slimy baby was lying on the floor shaking its head.

Since he was at the farm anyway, I thought I would just have him take a look at another cow that was not eating well. It did not take him long to make the diagnosis. A displaced abomasum, though, was not something he wanted to deal with while his supper was waiting. Besides, Daddy and Paul were not around to help at the moment, and they were needed to try this new method of treating a twisted stomach. Some brilliant idealist had come up with the idea that if the cow could just be turned upside down, the air-filled displaced stomach would float back up to its appropriate place. Then it would be a relatively simple operation to slip a couple of stitches through the belly wall into the stomach and tie it down. This would correct the problem without the need to perform an open operation. The idea seems reasonable until one considers that a cow weighs one thousand pounds, has four legs, and really has no desire to be turned upside down. Therefore, manpower is of essence—along with some skill.

I tell Daddy and Paul at breakfast that the vet is coming this morning and that we will need their help to turn the cow over. I make my way to the barn after breakfast and clean in the parlor while I wait for the vet's arrival. I am getting cold, though, so I decide to return to the house to read the newspaper while I wait. Just before noon, I see his truck finally roll up to the milk house. I look for Daddy and Paul, but they are nowhere to be found. Joseph says that they went to town. Great! The dialogue in my head is angry. *They knew the vet was coming and they ran off anyway. This is March, so there is nothing that they are doing that can't wait. Their stuff is always more important than helping with the cows."*

Joseph, Dr. Groves, and I come up with a system to make the turn with just the three of us. First, Dr. Groves will wrap a lasso around the cow in front of her back legs. Pulling on this has the effect of causing the cow to bow down onto her stomach. Joseph will grab the head, I will grab the front feet, and the vet will take the back feet. We twist and turn and pull numerous times until we get the cow unto her back and situated along the edge of the concrete in the slatted floor barn. This is to try to hold her in the correct position. All three of us are covered in manure, sweaty, and in a foul mood before we finally get the job accomplished.

Daddy and Paul appear as the veterinarian is cleaning up his utensils. I am still angry, and I spit out at them, "You knew he was coming, and you just ran away anyway. You could help once in a while."

Daddy scowls and responds in kind, "I have things to do too. I can't sit around all day waiting for the vet."

I rarely express my feelings to Daddy because I have learned that there is no empathy when I do express myself—only lecturing in return. But today, my anger motivates me to say what I would normally stuff inside. The result is that I feel guilty for not being the nice, submissive daughter I am supposed to be, while at the same time being angry that my position is never heard.

I don't feel like doing anything more, so I retire to my bedroom to sleep for the rest of the day as a black cloud descends over me. I go out of my way to avoid Daddy for the next two days and spend most of the time in my bedroom, except during milking. I do not want to see him or talk to him. It's not too difficult a thing to avoid Daddy because he doesn't come to help milk much anymore anyway.

On the third day, the vet comes again to do another twisted stomach. Daddy must have called him. I glance out the window and see the familiar blue truck parked at the barn but decide that I am not going out today. I am still fuming and disappointed in everyone.

"Why aren't you helping at the barn?" Mama asks when she gets up from her nap.

I just shrug. "They don't really need me."

"You better go out." She insists several times.

I see she is not going to leave me alone, so I pull on my coat and head out. The whole process of tacking the stomach down on an upside down cow goes much better with the help of more hands. With the departure of the vet, Daddy sees his chance.

"It's about time you straighten up. I bought this farm for you children, so stop pouting about all the work. You think you are so much better than all the rest of us. I won't put up with your attitude, so get over it."

Another layer is added to my growing resentment. *If this is our farm, how come we don't have any say in it?"*

The cool rainy days of March and April have given way to the warm sun of May. It is time to plant corn again. Daddy and Paul have moved ahead with plans for the planting season. Daddy and Mama have been spending considerable time searching for money for financing, and Daddy has every confidence that he will succeed. I have never known Daddy to give up until he gets where he wants to go.

In looking at options, though, Daddy decided that if the farm did sell here in Minnesota, he would like to move to Texas. In keeping with this plan, on April 6, he and a real estate agent that he had befriended left for a four-day trip to Texas to scout out the possibilities there. They returned with mixed reports of lots of farmland but unfortunately also a need to irrigate a lot of it.

I awake today to the patter of raindrops on the window. There will be no planting today. It is the middle of May, and planting has been going well, with everyone concentrating on getting the corn in the ground. Between milkings, I have been spending my time working ground with the four-wheel-drive tractor and hauling fertilizer in the gravity-box truck. This has taken my time away from the cows, so today I need to play catch-up. My first priority is to take the bull calves to the sale barn. On the way home, I maneuver the pickup and gooseneck trailer into the small space at the feed mill in town. I need to pick up some bagged minerals to mix into the cow feed, as Joseph needs them today for the weekly grinding. The roar of the tractor propelling the feed grinder greets me when I pull into the farm yard. I catch a glimpse of Daddy emerging from the house to help with unloading. As I open the tailgate on the trailer, I turn just in time to see Daddy slam Joseph against the tractor tire. His face is contorted into angry lines, and he is shouting.

"Why are you using the 4010? You know you are only supposed to use the 3010 for grinding feed. You don't listen to anything I tell you."

This is not the first time I have seen this behavior, but it has been increasing. I do not understand why he hates Joseph. I despise Daddy when he loses control like this, but I feel powerless to do anything.

Joseph glares back at him.

"You're just in your second childhood," he growls, then he turns and walks away.

In silence, I help unload the minerals. My stomach is now in knots, and I just want to escape to the barn.

The weather in early July is hot. The crops are growing well. Just after breakfast, a semi-truck with a drop-deck trailer pulls into the farm yard bearing a Caterpillar. Soon the air is filled with the sounds of the growling engine, followed by cracking wood and the thunk of falling trees. The trees are being ripped out to make way for a new grain setup.

Within the last month, Daddy has been successful in finding a loan company that is willing to finance the farm. He has wasted no time in paying off the contract for the deed and making the back payments with our former loan agency. The loan agency told him when he went to make the payment that they were planning a sheriff's sale for July 1. That was a close call. The farm has been saved in the nick of time. Daddy also cancelled the contract with the real estate agency to sell the farm.

With the immediate financial crisis resolved, Daddy is moving full steam ahead in developing the farm. Another twenty-thousand-bushel grain bin has been ordered and also a holding bin to put the wet corn into. This will be placed above the dryer. These additions will greatly increase the efficiency of harvest by eliminating the need to wait to unload. Daddy has also given the go-ahead to the tiling company to tile the currently non-tillable land. This is planned for August.

The month of July has sped by. Today, the last day of July, the sun is warm, but the air feels cooler than the past weeks. Joseph has been spending his days "walking beans." We have two hundred acres of soybeans and, because we alternate crops from year to year when possible, the field where the beans are growing this year was planted in corn last year. The result is that a lot of volunteer corn comes up with the beans. Corn in with the beans is not looked upon highly and will result in the farmer being "docked" in price for his product. Weed sprays do not kill corn. Therefore, "walking beans" to hand-pull all of the volunteer corn from the soybeans has become a standard practice in this area. Joseph has been working on this every day for a couple of weeks, but he is making little progress. To speed up the process, Daddy has decreed that Paul and I are to help him today.

Joseph and I bounce around in the bucket of the backhoe

while Paul speeds along the field drive that snakes across the middle of the farm to the field at the north end. The rows stretch away into the distance. This field is one-quarter of a mile long. I am not in the mood for this at all, but I do feel sorry for Joseph. He is made to do most of the labor-intensive jobs alone.

Paul maintains his position on the backhoe. His idea of helping is giving Joseph and me a ride between the patches of the stalwartly standing green stalks scattered out all over the landscape. As we move along the rows, I pull stalk after stalk, until my hands are covered with green and brown and rivulets of sweat streak down my back. By noon, we have done sixteen rows, hardly making a dent in this huge field. I am tired, and I ache. Paul decides he has had enough of this too. Joseph and I agree wholeheartedly. Daddy and Mama have gone to town and won't know when we quit anyway. I am so tired that I sleep until milking time.

Daddy and Mama do not return from town until we are partway through the evening milking. Daddy walks though the parlor without looking in my direction at all. The parlor exit door slams as he steps out into the free-stall barn, making his way to the feed room, halfway down the stalls. He spies Joseph leaning on the gate, staring out the open western barn door. Joseph is supposed to be chasing the next group of cows around for milking. I step out of the parlor to chase a straggler in from the holding area. I glance up to see Daddy walk up behind Joseph and kick him in the behind.

"Get to work. It's no wonder you can't get anything done. All you do is stand around and dream. You're just plain lazy."

I don't know what he is trying to prove, but I wish he would quit it. *Why can't we just be nice to each other?*

Later, as we gather at the table for supper, tension is thick in the air, and Daddy is still spewing words of contempt toward Joseph. His tirade culminates with, "You are just plain useless."

Mama sits quietly and says nothing. I finally gather up my courage and ask the question that has been troubling me.

"Why do you hate Joseph?"

The denial is instant. "I don't hate him. He just needs to learn to work and do as he is told."

I glance at Daddy's scowling face. *Well, you could have fooled me, and I don't believe that for one minute.* I do not dare voice this thought.

It is not until years later, after studying family systems, that I recognize the family roles each of us plays. These emerge clearly during the first couple of years in Minnesota. Daddy is the controller and has always been the controller. But our first disastrous crop year in Minnesota has magnified this trait. I don't know if he consciously determines that the only way to succeed is to control everything that everyone does, but that is how he begins to act. Paul has always been the firstborn son with generous privileges, but now he becomes the son who can do no wrong. I, as the middle child and only daughter, become the peacemaker and the pleaser. I want everyone to get along and live in peace, but I feel powerless. Finally, there has always been a noticeable attitude from Daddy that Joseph somehow does not deserve quite the same goodness as his other two children. This now springs forth in full force, with Joseph becoming the scapegoat of the family. All the anger for the things that have gone wrong becomes directed at him. And Mama, through her failure to stand up for what she must know to be right, becomes an enabler of Daddy's behavior.

The corn and the beans look great this year. It is mid-September, and the ears of corn are filling out and maturing. In fact, it looks like we are going to have a bumper crop. Daddy and Paul have been busy filling the silo these last two weeks. They have chopped about one hundred acres and are preparing to empty the manure pit again. Today, though, we are doing something different, and I am excited. Ben, a friend of ours, has asked Paul, Joseph, and me to go with him to Farm Fest '76 in western Minnesota. Farm Fest is a huge farm-themed day put on by various seed and farm equipment companies, during which they demonstrate their various products to the attendees. It is billed as the "largest agricultural show in Minnesota." The exhibits cover over fifty acres. We rush through milking and are ready when Ben picks us up around nine o'clock in the morning. I have butterflies in my stomach and a song in my heart.

The whole day is an adventure for me. I don't think I have ever seen so many cars in one place before. Parallel lines of multicolored cars, intermingled with the green strips of alfalfa, cover the hayfield parking lot. People mill everywhere. I notice that the policemen patrolling the crowd get to ride horses. That looks like a fun job. I wonder what it would be like to ride a horse. I have always wanted one, but Daddy says they are just hay burners. They don't make any money. We stop to watch the tractor-pull. I love the noise and the smoke. What a sense of power! Later, I see that the Budweiser Company has its forty-horse hitch on display in the afternoon, and I beg to stay to see it. I am simply amazed that someone can actually control this many beautiful, powerful animals all at one time. I wonder what would happen if they all started to run at once. Before I know it, it is time to head home, for the cows are waiting. I am tired, and my legs ache from all the walking, but I am happy.

I quickly change clothes when we arrive home and head for the barn. We are late getting started with the milking. Oh well, to me it was worth it. But I need to take a deep breath and remind myself to hold my tongue, as there is a price to pay for our day of fun.

"During harvest is not the time to go running off for the day. We should have been working today to get the crops in." Daddy scolds us all at the supper table.

We eat in silence. There will be no sharing of the day's events.

The month of January in the year of 1977 has slid into eternity, and February is upon us. The temperatures have moderated from the subzero thirties of a month ago. Snowflakes drift down from the starless sky into the glow of the yard light. My eyelids are still heavy as I stumble toward the barn in my half-sleep state. Another day in another year has begun, and the cows are waiting for their morning milking.

After milking, I check on the pregnant cows before heading in for breakfast. Daddy has bought another group of six first-calf heifers that will be freshening (calving) any day. I see one that looks like she might calve today, but I decide that I will come back out later. The pen needs cleaning out before I can move her, and I don't want to spend the time right now. I am feeling a little more lighthearted today, as I don't really need to do much in the barn.

My little dab of oatmeal and my shoofly pie await me. If it weren't for Mama's shoofly pie, I think I would skip breakfast. Daddy is smiling at breakfast, and I relax. Daddy has been invited to a Dekalb banquet tonight to receive a plaque for having the top corn yield in the county. The crop yield last fall would be the dream of any farmer, but Daddy was especially pleased since our first year was so dismal. The corn weighed in at one hundred thirty-six bushels per acre, and the soybeans figured out at sixty-one bushels per acre. This is not bad for a Minnesota transplant.

I bundle into my barn clothes after breakfast and make a beeline for the barn. I fork out the old straw, wash out the pen, and re-bed with fresh straw. It looks fresh and inviting for its new occupant.

"Joseph," I call, "Can you help me get this heifer in?"

He is busy pushing silage out to the heifers with the wheelbarrow but meanders over. Together, we dash back and forth, trying to coax—or maybe the correct terminology is force—this animal to cooperate with us and enter the clean, warm barn to have her baby. We are finally successful in our endeavor, and she is left to work on having her baby. Her pelvic muscles have dropped, and her tail is already elevated, indicating that she is well into labor. I am concerned though, as she is a very small heifer. If the calf is very big, she will not be able to have it. But there is no use standing around waiting to see what will happen, so I return to the house.

"Can you type my *Budget* letter today? And when you get a chance, you can do the income and expense figures for January too," Mama suggests.

Not a problem. I love math, and Mama has been having me put that bookkeeping class I did for Paul to good use. Mama's manual typewriter from college is soon positioned on the desk, and I slide a sheet of blank paper between its rollers. I am glad too that I took typing in ninth grade, before I quit school. Soon my fingers are dancing across the keys, and the words to Mama's *Budget* letter appear. Mama has been writing about our experiences for the weekly paper to keep our friends and family informed of our life. I miss the people I grew up with. There are many days when I am just lonely. I proofread the letter before sliding it into the mailing envelope. It does sound like these people have a very interesting and exciting life. If only it were really like it sounded.

I move on to typing some refinancing papers for Mama and Daddy and then gather up the milk check receipts and paid bills receipts. I pencil the income into one column and the bills into another. One of the bills for the farm now is a two-hundred-dollar-per-month payment to each of us. Daddy and Mama have decided that, as a tax write-off, this year they will begin paying each one of us this amount. Then we are to pay them back half of the amount as room and board. The remaining one hundred dollars is ours to keep. I have been diligently putting the money into a savings account for safekeeping. It really doesn't seem like much pay, but our basic needs and health care are paid for, and Daddy promises that if we all work together on the farm, we will receive our fair share in the end. I feel important to be asked to help with the books, and it gives me a sense of belonging to be able to know what is happening financially.

As I bend over the financial records, I hear the familiar barking outside that alerts me to the arrival of someone. I turn to glance out the window. A county sheriff deputy steps out of his car and walks toward the house. *Not again!* I open the door to his knock. Daddy is not home, so I accept the notice that he extends to me. The notice is to inform us that the real estate agent is suing us for the commission on the listing of the farm. Daddy may have cancelled the sale contract, but the agent still wants his one-hundred-thousand-dollar commission, just as if he had sold the farm.

The bookkeeping all done, I am eager to finish the dress that I have been making. I like to sew, and since one cannot just go to a store and buy a cape dress of the style that is worn by Mennonite women, I have learned to make my own. That way, at least I can choose the material and the style that I like. Puffy sleeves and frilly things are not my style, but I do like the jeans look. Since I can't actually wear blue jeans, I have learned to sew my skirt seams like those on the edges of jean legs, creating my own distinctive style. I just need to attach the collar to the blue plaid I am working on, and I will be done with this one. Putting the collar on is one of the harder pieces of making a dress. The material curves and tends to bunch up as the pressure foot comes around with the stitching. But after a couple of tries, the finished result does not look too bad.

By the time I win the dress battle, it is almost time to milk again. I need to go out a little early to check on the calving heifer. I peer over the planks on the side of the pen. It doesn't take me long to realize that the feet sticking out of the little heifer are those of a half-grown cow. I think this one is more than I can handle. I make the phone call and then begin the milking routine until the veterinarian arrives.

Dr. Grove's reaction is the same as mine.

"Wow, those are big feet. I will put the calf puller on and see if maybe we can pull the calf, but I am guessing we are going to have to do a C-section. If it were dead, we could cut it in pieces, but it looks like it is still alive."

Cutting up a calf into pieces sounds like a gruesome task, but doing a Cesarean section on a cow sounds equally challenging. We first hook the calf puller to the two huge feet and begin to slowly winch. But the calf is firmly wedged and will not budge. It is time to move on to the C- section. This is something I have never done, and I find it intriguing. While Joseph continues with the milking, I gather the requested items: a bucket of water and a straw bale for our operating table. The heifer is exhausted from her efforts at expelling the calf. She sprawls out on her right side in the middle of the pen. After a good scrubbing with antiseptic and the liberal local injection of lidocaine, Dr. Grove carefully makes a cut across the side of the animal. The uterus, with its load of calf, soon moves back and forth under the open slit.

"We have to move fast once I make the cut into the uterus. I will try to find the hind feet and then you will have to lift it out," instructs the vet.

I watch the glistening black and white appear and reach for the feet that Dr. Groves shoves my way. The slimy feet slip though my fingers, and I lose my grip. This is not working well. I grab some twine and loop it around so I have handles. Then we both lift for all we are worth. Picking a one-hundred-pound, slippery calf straight up out of a narrow hole takes all my strength, but soon the calf is lying on the floor shaking its head. The poor mother just lies there, panting, with a huge hole in her side. Dr. Groves begins the tedious task of sewing the uterus and skin incision back together while I watch. Our milking routine has been totally thrown off during this hour-and-a-half operation, and it is one thirty in the morning when I finally fall into bed.

Daddy and Mama have gone to town, to the loan agency. No one is around to ask any questions, so I pick up the scrap of paper lying on my bureau. It contains the phone number Cory has given me. A couple of weeks ago, Cory, my friend from high school, stopped by to visit me. She and a friend were on their way to California. We talked and laughed about old times. She ended her visit by inviting me to go along to California with her. I hesitated but then shrugged and declined because, in the back of my mind, I knew that I'd never be allowed to go. But the phone number stares me in the face, and the thought is tantalizing. I pick up the phone and dial the number. I tell Cory that I want to come to California. But now I have a problem. How am I ever going to convince Daddy?

Daddy moves from cow to cow, washing udders and placing the milkers on. He is silent, but the lines on his face are relaxed. I decide to take the dive.

"Daddy, Cory wants me to come to California to visit for a week. Can I go? Please, just to get away for a little."

His jaw sets and the facial lines tighten.

"Your place is here on the farm, not running all over the country with someone who is going to lead you into who knows what. I can't do all this work by myself."

That was pretty much the answer I was expecting, but I am still disappointed. At nineteen years of age, I am restless and am becoming increasingly more dissatisfied with the life that is mine. I beg Daddy a couple more times over the next day to let me go. He finally just says, "No, and that is final."

I reluctantly call Cory and tell her to "just forget it. Daddy is not going to let me go."

This place is hopeless. I just can't feel good toward him anymore. I struggle with my inner thoughts. Another voice in my head reminds me that I am to honor my father, and I really do believe in my heart that God will honor me if I do that. I have been quoted the Bible verse, "Children, obey you parents … Honor your father and mother," followed by the commentary of "this is the will of the Lord for you" more times than I care to remember. And it has been etched into my soul that in obeying one's father, one is obeying God—and obedience to God will be honored with blessing.

Chapter 6

TURNING POINT

*P*ain explodes through me, and I can feel myself spinning and falling. I instinctively know, as I kneel in the brown, slimy manure outside the cows' sickroom door, that I can't get up. I had come to the barn early to get a couple of cows in to breed, but one of the cows had other ideas. She did not want to cooperate. As I tried to get her to put her head into the stanchion, she turned and ran down the narrow alley beside the calving pen, headed for the door. Not to be outdone, I had run to head her off. I had always won before, so I did not think about what might happen if she were more determined than I. We both reached the door at the same time. I was hit with a powerful blow that I felt only as pressure as I was crushed between her and the door.

I gasp for breath as I sit on the cold, wet, filthy concrete. Several times, I try to stand up, but my body does not respond. I know that I am seriously injured, but I have no idea how to get help.

"Help! Help!" I call several times, but my voice only echoes back at me in the eerie expanse of the barn. I seriously doubt that anyone can hear me, and I am not about to sit here until

someone finally comes to find me. I make the decision to crawl
out of the barn. As I drag my right leg behind my left up the
alley and into the sickroom, I realize that the other cow that I
was getting in is still standing there. Now she is freaked by this
strange being and also decides to make a dive for the door. A
sense of terror fills me as I realize that I am now at risk of being
stepped on as she frantically makes her escape. I know that I
need to stand up if I am going to save myself from such a fate.
Adrenalin surges through me as I grip the pen sideboard, and
my arm muscles strain to lift the weight I cannot support with
my legs. It's not a second too soon; I am clinging to the pen rail-
ing as she rushes by. *Now that I am up, maybe I can walk.* I take
one step and realize that there is no support, only overwhelming
pain. With a cry, I lower myself back to the floor and begin again
my painstaking crawl. Over the next fifteen minutes, I slowly
drag myself through the parlor, the milk house, and finally out
the milk-house door. I spy Joseph by the heifer barn with the
silage-filled wheelbarrow.

"Help me," I gasp.

A clatter of metal is followed by running footsteps. Joseph's
concerned face soon peers down at me. "What happened?"

"Just go get Daddy," is all I can say, and he sprints away to
the house. It seems like an eternity before Joseph returns with
Daddy and Paul.

"Go get Mama," Daddy instructs Paul, "and I'll get the
pickup."

"Amanda is badly hurt," are the words Mama hears as Paul's
frantic voice arouses her from her afternoon sleep, sleep that she
needs before beginning her nightly shift at the hospital.

He bounds back down the stairs, and I soon hear the pickup
truck backing up to me. I grit my teeth as Daddy and Paul lift
me onto the pickup tailgate and drive slowly toward the house.

"We need to change her dress," Daddy says to Mama, who by now has gotten dressed and rushed out to meet us.

"No. No. We don't take time for that," Mama insists.

I know I look a sight, but at this point, I really don't care what I look like. "Just get me to the hospital," is my only request.

Together, Paul and Daddy lift me into the backseat of the car. I find that if I lie on my left side, the pain is less, but the bouncy car ride is still torture. I am nauseated, and I break out in a sweat. This second day of June 1977 is not turning out at all like I envisioned.

"I think we will let you go home today," are Dr. Schaefer's opening words to me as he steps into my hospital room on my tenth day in the hospital. His bearded face smiles down at me as he waves toward the door.

X-rays on my arrival showed pelvic fractures in two places on the right. Because of the location of the fractures, there was a great concern that my urinary system might also be damaged. This would have required surgery, but that concern has proved unfounded. I have spent most of my time in bed, though, unable to do much of anything for myself. I have never realized before that sitting up requires the use of so many muscles that are attached to the pelvis. For the first few days, I moved only when the nurses came to log-roll me to change the sheets or lift me onto a cart to go to X-ray. I did not have the strength to roll over in bed by myself or to sit up. I felt weepy and depressed, but my days were brightened by the visits of church people and the beginning influx of numerous get-well cards and flowers.

I don't think I have had this much attention in all of my life. I also am touched by the kindness and gentleness of the nurses who care for me every day, and a seed is planted that will influence my life in the days to come. I have always said that I would never be a nurse like my mother, but my view has begun to change as a result of this experience. If caring for others in a spirit of generosity and joyfulness is what nursing is all about, I find it enticing. Realizing that this is what my mother does every day implants a certain respect for her in my heart that wasn't there before.

The house seems far too quiet, and everything looks different on my arrival home. I am lightheaded and woozy. I can use crutches to get around, but I am not to put any weight on my right leg. I collapse into bed, exhausted. My afternoon is spent listening to records, sleeping, and reading. It seems strange to not have to go to the barn to milk or take care of the cows.

June slides into July. My days over the last four weeks have taken on a common pattern. I awaken today to the chirping of birds outside my open, screened window. The midsummer sun is shining. The clock reads 6:00 a.m. I feel rested for the first time in my life. I can't believe how good it feels to not have to get up at four every morning to milk. My muscles, though, still will not allow me to sit up in bed without assistance. I have developed a method of rolling over first and then pushing up from the side of the bed as I slide my legs out. I reach for the crutches that are lying on the other bed in my room and make my way to the bathroom. Getting dressed is a slow process, but I have the house to myself and all the time in the world.

After breakfast, I choose a fun project for the day. Since my accident, I have been inundated with cards and gifts from friends far and near. The young ladies my age from our former church in Pennsylvania have sent a homemade scrapbook and a sunshine box full of puzzles, books, and crafts to keep me occupied. I am truly overwhelmed by all the generosity. I didn't know that so many people cared about me. A five-thousand-piece puzzle of an old mill in autumn looks like an interesting project, and I spread it out on the table in our mostly unused sitting room. Sorting pieces and laying out what looks like the border pieces occupies me for a couple of hours while Mama takes her nap and then goes to the garden to pick peas.

Around eleven o'clock in the morning, I hear the front door close and Mama's always cheery voice.

"Can you come and help me shell the peas?"

I leave my puzzle and make my way to the kitchen. Soon, my fingers are splitting the pods and popping out the luscious green peas. By three o'clock, most of the peas are shelled and tucked away in the refrigerator. I am ready now for some outdoor time. It is then that I notice the milk truck backed up to the milk house. *Good!* Bernie, the portly, jovial milk hauler, loves to talk, and I hobble my way on crutches to the barn. Friendly banter flows for well over half an hour before Bernie needs to climb up into his cab and move on to his next stop. I wave good-bye and return to the house to work on a new dress. It seems strange not to be out milking at 4:00 p.m. and by 6:00 p.m., I feel compelled to wander out. Basically, all I can do is watch and offer my advice. I really can't do much, and my book is calling. I return to the house. The porch swing beckons, and I sit and read as the warm summer breeze touches my face. Tomorrow, July 15, will be my return doctor appointment, and I am anxious as to what he will say.

X-rays are done, and Mama and I wait, filled with anticipation, for Dr. Schaeffer in his office. He offers a handshake and a grin as he pushes his slight form through the doorway.

"Stand up, and let's see you walk."

I am not so sure about this, but I do as he says. My "walk"

turns out to be more of a drunken swagger as I attempt to get my right leg to follow the left as I make my way from one side of the office to the other.

"Just go home, and take it slow. You're young, and you shouldn't need any therapy," are his final instructions.

I am thrilled to be mobile again. The first thing I do when I get home is hop on my bicycle and pedal around the farmstead. The wind in my face as I sail along is exhilarating.

Another week goes by before my leg is strong enough to allow me to gradually start helping to milk in the evenings again. I really have no desire to pick up where I left off. This summer has been the most relaxing I have spent since I was a small child. I have been removed from the friction of daily living, and the constant tension that I was feeling has evaporated. I have actually had time to just sit and enjoy the small pleasures of reading a book, doing a puzzle, or chatting with friends without needing to feel guilty about not being productive enough. Daddy seems genuinely concerned for my well-being and has not criticized me for not being available to help. I have been able to spend some time away from the farm with other youth from church. And I have not needed to listen to the constant derogatory putdowns of Joseph that cause my stomach to curl into a tight knot. I didn't know it was possible to enjoy life so much.

By now, it is late July, and Daddy is busy during the day hauling last year's corn to the river by tractor-trailer to be loaded onto barges. He has contracted it for delivery during June, July, and August in order to make room for this coming season's crop. His day begins with doing the milking in the morning and then he swings into the Mack truck to begin the two daily round trips of about two hundred miles each to the Mississippi River terminal.

I spend my time today helping my ever-industrious Mama can sweet corn. The ears of corn wait in boxes for my hands to pull their green skirts off, one by one, to expose the plump yellow rows beneath. Once there are a couple of dozen ears lying naked, it is time to slice the juicy kernels into a pan. I soon develop a blister on my index finger from repeatedly drawing the knife over the cob to strip away its glistening harvest. The clock on the wall marks the slow, methodical progress of the day. I glance up as I hear the descending whine of the truck engine. Daddy is rolling past the house on his way back from the second load. It is 3:30 p.m. and time for milking.

"You had better go." Mama's words release me from my current task.

I am happy to leave Mama to finish the canning by herself. But when I get to the barn, the milkers still sit undisturbed in their wash racks, and the cows chew their cuds lazily in their stalls. No one has started the milking chores. I soon realize that any thought that things might have changed during my time of being unable to work can be discarded.

Over the last year, we have started to occasionally attend church with another Mennonite group that has been attempting to get established about thirty-five miles northwest of here. As they do not have a church building, the group is meeting in the basement of one of the homes for now. Daddy and Mama still have hopes of starting a group closer to us, but that is starting to look more and more like an unattainable dream. I enjoy this new group and look forward to Sundays there. However, getting to church on time has added a new dynamic of chaos to Sundays. Because of the distance, we need to plan for an hour of driving time, which means that we need to be on the road by eight thirty.

My watch reads 7:10 a.m. as the milk-house door slams behind me. I can hear the rattle of the bunk feeder. Daddy is feeding the cows with the automated belt feeder, and Paul is just finishing up with hauling out the manure. Joseph is feeding the heifers and then he is expected to scrape all the stalls before he is done. The oatmeal is bubbling by the time Daddy and Paul come in and we sit down to eat. We do not wait for Joseph.

"He could move faster if he wanted to. We're not going to wait for him all our lives," Daddy grumbles.

I can feel the knot forming in my stomach as I feel the tension rising. I escape to my room as soon as possible to change clothes and take a nap if I have time. The clock reads 8:30 by the time I finally hear the slam of the mudroom door announcing Joseph's arrival to the house. Daddy strides toward the kitchen, his posture rigid and his mouth set in a firm line. He is on the rampage now. He roars.

"You do this on purpose. You'll never amount to anything if you don't start moving faster. No son of mine acts this way. It's about time you grow up."

Joseph, a solid, well-built eighteen-year-old, strolls through the kitchen past Daddy and up the stairs without making eye contact or acknowledging him. The rest of us make our way to the car, where we sit and wait. The digital clock in the car has flipped to 8:40 a.m. by the time Joseph finally shuffles toward the car. The ride to church is one of total silence.

Sunday school is already underway when we arrive. We slip into our pew as quietly as possible. An hour of Sunday school is followed by the singing of several hymns and then a message by the minister, Alvin Schmutz, from the Bible. I allow my mind to drift and my eyes to flicker during the forty-five minute sermon. The smell of delicious food floats my way.

Laughter and banter are free-flowing around the tables as we partake of the various hot dishes supplied by the ladies for the potluck lunch. There are several visiting families from other locales, which swells the number of those partaking to around forty today.

A Bible game appears after the food is put away. This is soon interrupted by the young boys who want to play softball. I always loved playing softball in high school and am soon pulled into the play. I really have not done much running since I broke my pelvis and find that my right leg is still weak. By the time I have run around the bases a couple of times, I am limping and have developed a sharp pain in my groin. But by now, it is time to go home anyway. The cows are waiting.

"What is taking you so long?" Daddy shouts up the stairs. "You need to get out there so Paul can go plow."

The cows are milked, and I am hurrying to get my hair combed. My stomach is already tied in a knot, and weariness envelopes me. The sky is overcast, the air is damp, and with each step, my shoes collect an additional layer of mud as I hurry out of the house on this mid-November day to the corn dryer. During the last few weeks, we have had rain every few days, making picking and hauling corn frustrating. I am tired of the struggle every day that seems never-ending. The yield looks good, though, and Daddy and Paul have prepared for the harvest by buying two more twenty-thousand-bushel grain bins. Daddy continued to haul corn to the river while Paul, Joseph, and I spent a couple of weeks in September putting them together and pushing their shiny silver sides up into the sky. Now, there are three large bins that wait to be filled with the bountiful harvest. Once the bins were up and the silo-filling completed, we were finally able to start picking corn on October 12.

The dryer is already running and the 14-percent-moisture corn is dribbling into the Chevy truck as I walk up. Monitoring the dryer is my job today, along with switching the trucks after they fill with dry corn. The tractor pulling a gravity wagon loaded with corn rolls to a stop beside me and Joseph jumps off.

"Can you help me switch wagons?" he asks.

The gravity box parked at the dryer has been slowly feeding into the auger system each time the dryer "calls" for more corn. Now it is time to park a full one there and take the empty one away. The dryer has not been drying fast enough, though, to allow Daddy to keep combining continuously using this method alone. Between gravity-box swaps, Paul has put Joseph to work making a wet corn pile behind the storage bins. This corn will be dried later.

By the time we have gotten the wagons switched, the dry corn truck is full and needs to be emptied. I usually like harvesting in the fall, but I find this year to be completely taxing and depressing. I put the truck in second gear and push the accelerator to the floor. Two-inch-deep tracks appear in the new gravel underlay around the bins as I make my slow crawl to the auger for unloading. I do not dare stop or the truck, with its load, will sink into the soft ground, making it impossible to get moving again. I roar around the bin and make my swing to get into position to back up to the auger that will accept the corn for movement into the new storage bin. The trick now is to be able to back up to the auger without stalling the truck five times and stop at exactly the right place without really being able to see where the screener and auger are. One morning a week ago, Joseph was backing up the truck, and he smashed the screener because he didn't get stopped soon enough. A half-day of harvesting was lost getting parts to fix it. Daddy was angry and scolded Joseph.

"You're just so stupid and careless. You think you're so good, and you can't do anything right."

Later in the evening, after dark, Joseph was backing up again to unload and smashed it again. Needless to say, Daddy spewed some more rather unkind, loudly delivered, demeaning dialogue. So now I am tense every time I back up to the auger because I don't want to be stupid and worthless too.

By mid-afternoon, the combine has broken down, and Paul is designated to work on fixing it while Daddy decides to take a load of corn to the river. Joseph will watch the wagons and trucks and take care of the heifers. I am left to milk alone. I sigh as I make my way to the milk house. I have returned to the "rat race" full time. I am forever tired, and I really want to do something with my life other than milk cows. Having the summer off from constantly working has made me realize that there is another world out there, a world that I want to be a part of. Though I don't totally realize it at the time, this past summer has become a turning point in my life. In my mind, I am able to crystallize the direction that I want my life to take. Instead of being a veterinarian, I have shifted my interest to people. I decide that I can do the same things I love and not have to try to push and pull one-thousand-pound patients around. My decision is not something I verbalize because I know it will not be accepted by my father.

Chapter 7

TRAPPED—FRUSTRATION SETS IN

*T*he wind drives the cold thorough my thin Sunday overcoat as I hurry out to the car. I shiver. It is fifteen degrees below zero on this wintery January morning, but I am looking forward to the day. We are headed for church at the recently acquired vacant school building in Hansville, Minnesota, a small town about thirty miles from our farm. The building has been purchased by a group of Midwestern Mennonite churches that have banded together into an organized fellowship network. The express purpose of the purchase is to start a winter Bible school for conservative Mennonite teenagers and young adults. The inadvertent benefit for the emerging Mennonite group near Moorland—and consequently also for us— is that church services can now be held at the school, in the chapel. I cannot believe our good fortune in having our community chosen for this new school. I am excited about the prospects.

The chapel lies just off to the right as we enter the north door of the building. The service begins at ten. I look around at the families, seated together, lifting up their voices to God in four-part harmony. The music is beautiful, and I feel at home. After the service, I wander through the building looking at the progress being made with the renovations. Bible school starts in just four weeks, on February 5, 1978, so all the work needs to be done by then. As I walk around, a longing rises in me. *If only I could go to Bible school. It sounds like a heap of fun.* I immediately push the wistful thoughts back down. *Daddy would never allow us to go.*

Later in the day, Daddy comes into the parlor to help Joseph and me finish up the milking. I address his back as he preps a cow.

"I really want to go to Bible school. Please, can Joseph and I go this winter?"

I hold my breath and busy myself with a milker, not daring to look at him. I can feel his piercing eyes on me.

"I can't run this farm all by myself. We have work to do here. What's the matter with you guys that you want to go running off all the time? Sometimes I wish I had never had any children. If you really need to go to Bible school, you can go during the day. I still expect that you will help with the chores in the morning and evening and get the rest of your work done. The things they do in the evening are just silliness anyway."

I was expecting a flat out "no," so this is better than I had hoped for, but I am still stung by his words. Being told that we are such a burden that he wishes he had never had us are the most hurtful words a young person will ever hear. I intellectually hope that he doesn't really mean it, but subconsciously, I have begun to assimilate this message into who I am. Needless to say, Joseph and I grasp at the reluctant, half-hearted permission and send in our applications, indicating that we will only be attending classes during the day.

I awaken to the sound of the wind as it whines around the corner of the house. I groan. *Is the weather going to be too bad again today?* Yesterday, it snowed all day, and Joseph and I were advised to stay home. I really did not want to miss our fourth day of Bible school classes but finally decided maybe it was not wise to risk our lives. I was disappointed, though, and frustrated.

By the time we are done with milking, I decide that we are going to try it today. The driving falls to me since Joseph, at nineteen years of age, has not been allowed by Daddy to get a driver's license. Daddy says he is too careless and irresponsible to have a license. The snow flows across the road, driven by the westerly wind. It leaves growing white tufts in its wake. There are repeating thuds as the car bounces over the edges of drift after drift. The tires slide with each application of the brakes. At least it is not snowing. I drive slowly because I do not want to end up in the ditch again. Every muscle in my body is tense. Just three evenings ago, on the way home from Bible school, I spun the car into a snow bank at the end of our drive. Thankfully, Joseph was able to push me out. The last thing we wanted was for Daddy to know about that little misadventure.

Chapel is already underway by the time we arrive. After chapel, we disperse to our classes. I have a class on the book of Acts, one on the books of I & II Timothy and Titus, and one in child study. I am behind due to our missed day. I have several chapters to read in Acts for homework and an essay to write for each class over the next couple of weeks. In theory, we have the weekends and evenings to work on this, but for Joseph and me, there is no free time. There will be cows to milk and dairy chores we have been neglecting to catch up on. By study hall, I am feeling overwhelmed with the coursework. I decide instead of studying to hang out in the dorm and get to know some of the girls. The little voice in my head tells me that I am wasting a perfectly good hour and that I could be studying, but right now, but I am longing for social connection. I am starting to feel more comfortable just hanging around and watching the interactions, although I still feel totally out of the loop. I long to be one of the girls, but I find it hard to break into the friendship groups that have developed during their shared times in the evening. *I am such an outsider here. I feel like a total misfit. I hate this going back and forth, and I am never going to do it this way again.*

Whack! Whack! Whack! The Ping-Pong ball bounces back and forth. We have fifteen minutes to play while we wait for lunch to be served. I have finally gotten up the nerve to grab a paddle and actually play a game. It feels good. All too soon, the bell rings for lunch. The seating at the tables is such that the boys sit on one side of a table and girls sit on the other. I find myself seated across from a boy I especially admire. For just a moment, I allow myself to dream. *I wish I could get to know some of them (and especially him) better.* But there is no time for that since I am only here during class hours.

Three weeks fly by way too fast. Joseph and I missed a second day during the second week due to freezing rain. We were able to make it to classes on all the other days. I am exhausted from trying to "burn the candle" at both ends, but I have done it and there is a certain satisfaction in that. I have three As to show for my diligence and a few connections with many other young people of my faith. And I have made a decision that, somehow, I am going to go next year like everyone else does.

The sun's rays through the dining room window are getting shorter while their warmth is increasing. The thermometer reads seventy degrees. Though it is only the thirtieth of March, hope of spring is in the air. My spirits begin to lift with the sunshine and the warmth. It has been two weeks since the end of Bible school, and life has returned to its routine. I watch the pickup disappear down the driveway just after lunch. Daddy is off again to another pipeline meeting, this time in Iowa. He will not be back until tomorrow. Fighting the installation of an oil pipeline across the farm has become Daddy's preoccupation over the last four months. It came to our attention in mid-November that Williams Pipeline Company was planning on installing an eighteen-inch oil pipeline from the Twin Cities south into Iowa. The proposed route takes the pipeline right through the middle of the farm. This is not a project that any of us wants to see go through. Daddy, Mama, and Paul have been attending some kind of meeting at least once every week. There are informational meetings by Williams Pipeline Company, public hearings hosted by the State of Minnesota, and meetings by a protest group that has formed to fight the pipeline. Daddy has become highly involved in the protest group. And by doing so, he is walking on shaky ground in regard to the principles of nonresistance and nonconformity as taught and practiced by the Mennonite church.

"The Bible teaches clearly that those who belong to the kingdom of Christ are not of this world but are separate from it (in word and practice) ... In view of the teachings found in the scripture, there is no reason for Christian people to become aggressive parties to a lawsuit." reads the constitution and bylaws of the church. *"Members who violate these scriptures shall be held as transgressors."* Since the sole purpose of the protest organization is to stop the pipeline by using whatever means are necessary, involvement in it would be highly frowned upon by church leaders. But right now, saving the farm from a pipeline is what matters most to Daddy.

I pull a sweater over my head and head back out to the barn after milking. The four-wheel-drive 7520 John Deere sits by the farm fuel tank with the digger attached. Paul stands on the four-foot-high tractor tire, depressing the trigger on the diesel fuel nozzle as the liquid power gushes into the tank. He is getting ready to work the soil on this sunny first day in May, in preparation for the first planting of corn tomorrow. I weave my way between the digger and the new corn planter that graces the lawn as it waits to be put into service. Our lawn is not spared when the space is needed for the parking of equipment. This new planter allows for the use of liquid fertilizer instead of the dry we had previously used, and it has been purchased for that reason. I didn't really think we needed a new planter quite yet, but apparently Daddy thought we did.

Another rumble off to my left, behind the trees on the north side of the building site, reaches my ears. It is the sound of a Caterpillar as it drags a tiling attachment through four feet of black soil. The wetlands were tiled during our second year here, and now, a different tiling firm has been hired to turn the rest of our land into well-drained, productive soil. The tiling contractor has been working for the last couple of weeks to string and pull roll after roll of slotted, black, flexible plastic pipe into the ground. The hope is to get as much tiling done as possible today before planting begins tomorrow.

I hurry to wash out the cows' sickroom because I want to watch this operation while they are close to the buildings. It is mid-morning by the time I park my bicycle on the field drive just north of the windbreak and begin my vigil. For an hour or so, I watch the slow march of yellow across the field as the monster methodically swallows the black worm. Suddenly, black smoke snakes into the sky and the engine groans as the machine strains to make its way through an area of softer ground. I soon realize

that the Caterpillar is no longer moving forward, and the lower
edge of the track has disappeared from sight. The roar diminishes
to a low purr as the operator realizes he is hopelessly stuck in the
middle of a mud hole. *Uh Oh!* I have to assume that getting a
Caterpillar unstuck is not an easy task.

Before long, Paul, with the four-wheel-drive tractor, has been
summoned to help. He roars through the break in the trees and
backs up to the scene. But there is a problem. The Caterpillar is
too close to the windbreak at the end of the field to be able to get
a tractor on dry ground in front of him for pulling. Pulling him
backward or sideways would be impossible. A lengthy discussion
ensues before it is decided to hook onto the front of the Caterpillar
with a one-hundred-foot rope and then run it around a tree and
come off at a ninety degree angle to the tractor. It is a brilliant
plan, and in spite of some spinning on the part of our big tractor,
the Caterpillar soon inches out of the mud and up onto drier land.
Pieces of mud fly like missiles off the four tires as Paul speeds
away and back to his task. For me, it is time as well to return to
reality and put my hand to the task of milking the cows. I sigh.
There are lots of cows with mastitis again, and this results in extended time in the parlor and barn.

I hold my breath. *Do I dare take another breath?* I am lightheaded as I gaze upward into the hot September sun. Fear almost
paralyzes me as I watch Joseph, seated on the ball that dangles
from the end of a one-hundred-foot crane, lean out and try to
steady the upper section of the elevator leg. He clings to the cable
with one hand while using his other hand to try to steady the
swinging metal and put a bolt into the hole that will hold the
metal in its permanent position. There is no safety harness. One

slip by him or the crane operator and he will fall unimpeded to the ground below.

All through the month of August, Daddy and Paul have been working on this new elevator leg setup. When finished, the setup will greatly improve the speed and efficiency of harvest. First, in early August, there was cement to pour. A pad was poured for the dryer to sit upon, and alongside that, a concrete unloading area was constructed. Between the two areas will stand two separate legs. The smaller thirty-foot leg picks up the wet corn or beans that have been dumped off the truck into an auger embedded in the concrete. This leg then will empty into a holding bin that sits perched above the dryer. Gravity allows the holding bin's wet corn to fall into the dryer as needed. As it is dried, the corn is emptied into the main leg, which is one hundred feet tall. An elevator leg seems like a simple invention. It is simply two combined hollow tubes of metal that contain a revolving belt with plastic buckets attached. The buckets will lift the dry corn high into the air and then dump it for a free fall down one of the connecting pipes or downspouts to a waiting grain bin. Once it is completed, the setup will make harvesting a breeze and eliminate the bottlenecks.

Right now, though, as I watch the final piecing together of the tall-leg segments, I am terrified by what could happen. I am frightened especially for Joseph. The bottom section was easy enough. The ninety-foot lower segment was lifted off the ground and into place by the crane operator. Paul and Daddy only needed to place the bolts and tighten them on the ground. I was happy to do my part by staying on the ground and driving to town to get some cable clamps that Daddy had forgotten to buy. The top cap is a totally different story. The only way to put the two sections together is to bolt them together ninety feet up in the air. How to do that was the question of the day. The crane operator offered to give someone a ride up on the ball weight. Daddy and Paul looked at each other.

Daddy said, "One of you young ones needs to go up there."

And Paul responded. "Uh uh! I'm not riding that ball."

So Joseph was delegated to carry out the difficult and dangerous task. I am only too relieved when the bolts are in place, and Joseph is safely back on the ground. I am feeling nauseated. I pull in a huge breath of air and slowly release it. It has been a tense and trying day, but the end result is that we now have a modern grain storage facility.

I spray the udder of each cow in the lineup and return to wipe them dry with paper towels. While I do so, Daddy removes the milkers from the opposite row of cows. It is a Sunday evening in October. I am pleased that Daddy has come to help tonight. I glance up when I hear the sound of the vacuum pump change, indicating that someone has opened the milk-house door. I recognize the men who step through the door. They are the ministers of the Moorland Mennonite group. My interest is piqued. It is strange that they would come to visit unannounced and without their families. They spend a few minutes in casual conversation before they get to the point of their visit. They have come to talk to Daddy about the rumors that they are hearing regarding his involvement in the pipeline protest group. They spend most of the next couple of hours admonishing Daddy against his involvement and trying to help him see that this "unscriptural entanglement" with a worldly organization is in violation of the beliefs of the Mennonite church. They further request that he make a public statement to the church the following Sunday, confessing his involvement and assuring the church brethren that he will cease his participation in this activity. After their departure, the atmosphere is charged. Daddy has been incited.

"This is none of their business. If Ewert would have just kept his mouth shut, they wouldn't even know. Just because he couldn't make a go of it, he wants to make sure that I don't either. I'm going to do what I need to do to take care of my farm."

Daddy's tirade against the church's interference in his affairs engulfs our evening conversation and spills into the next day. Everyone in the family is pulled into the drama. I feel that we have no choice but to side with Daddy's view of the situation. Expressing an opinion otherwise would draw Daddy's scorn upon our own heads. But inside of me, my soul is distressed by the verbal outrage. I want to crawl into a hole somewhere and stay there. *Why does everything have to turn into a confrontation?*

Daddy approaches the podium the next Sunday to make his statement. My stomach is already in a knot, and a sharp pain is spreading outward. I just want to get up and run, but there is no place to run. Daddy begins. He admits that he has been fighting the installation of a pipeline across the farm but denies that what he is doing is wrong. He spends most of his time insisting that this is a private matter and that the church has no authority to be involved. "My heart before God does not condemn me," he finishes.

I can feel the heat rising into my face, and the shame of my father's inability to own any wrongdoing begins its creep into my identity. *I wish I could drop through the floor.*

Frost forms on my eyebrows, and the snow crunches with each step in the cold morning air. I sneak a peek at the thermometer on the garage as I make my way to the barn. It reads negative twenty-two degrees. Brr! January of 1979 has arrived in Minnesota. I hate working in the barn when it is so cold, but the appointment was made last week already for the veterinarian to come today and vaccinate calves for brucellosis. Brucellosis is a highly contagious bacterium that mostly causes abortion in cows, but when spread to humans, it can cause chronic disease in its host. We are required by federal law to vaccinate all calves before the age of six months for this disease. And because of the federal tracking requirements and the goal of eradicating this disease in the US, vaccination must be done by a veterinarian.

I greet Dr. Groves by his truck, and we place the vaccine, the tattoo pliers, needles, and a rope in a bucket to carry it to the old barn, where the heifers who need vaccinating reside. Dr. Groves nods toward the new structure that is expanding off of the current free-stall barn.

"Are you adding on?" he asks.

"Yeah. We're building a new free-stall barn. In this one, the stalls will be bedded with shavings instead of mats like we have in the old one. Daddy plans to milk up to two hundred cows. The high producers will get the new barn, and the dry cows and lower producers will get the old barn."

The dry cows currently live outdoors; having them indoors will certainly be a plus, as their teats often freeze when it is cold. This causes all kinds of headaches when they finally have their babies and start producing milk again. But I am frustrated by the continued push to milk more cows. The only comforting thought is that maybe we will have less mastitis if the higher-producing cows can lie in clean, dry stalls instead of on the always-damp mats in the older barn. The builders have been working on the new addition for several months now. The south side is already covered with tin, and the workers are slowly making progress on the north side and end when the weather is not too cold. However, the inside concrete pouring must wait until warmer weather.

Twelve calves mill around in the foot-deep, frozen manure of the twelve-foot-by-twelve-foot pen. The vet and I corner the first calf. Then I block the calf from backing up while Dr. Groves places the nose leader in its nose. Once the calf is tied, the vet gives the injection under the skin of her shoulder area in one quick motion. He then tattoos the calf's ear so that the animal has a permanent indication that it has been vaccinated. We move between the animals, having our feet stepped on, stumbling over the rough under-footing, and being crushed between animals until we have captured all twelve, one by one. At least, with all the moving about, only my fingers have become numb and no longer seem to be a part of my body.

With the calves all done, we move back to the free-stall barn to confirm whether pregnancies exist in fifteen cows that I have bred in the last couple of months. I have decided to get this task out of the way today too, while the vet is here, so that everything will be caught up when I leave for Bible school in just a couple of weeks.

I was able to talk Daddy into letting me actually go and stay for one three-week term this winter at the new Bible school twenty-five miles from us. I had waited to approach him with my request until he seemed to be in a cheerful mood one day while we were riding together to town to get a part. I knew too that if I asked for myself only, without Joseph being involved, I was more likely to receive a positive response. I recognize that I, at least, have some worthiness in my father's eyes that he, for whatever reason, does not grant to Joseph.

"All right," was his response, after a short pause as his brown eyes turned their piercing scrutiny on me. "Just this once. Then you need to get this nonsense out of your head. I need you at home to take care of the cows."

I am excited and looking forward to this time away. But I have

never shirked my duties. Therefore, I feel a need to have everything done so that Daddy and the boys don't need to do anything
extra while I am gone.

Here I am at Bible school. I like it here, and I hate it here. I have
been tense since I got here five days ago on Monday. *I don't feel like
I fit in anywhere, and I don't know how to enjoy myself like the others.*
Last night, the tightness in my stomach finally got the best of me,
and I threw up. I did not sleep well, and finally, I slipped out of
bed at my usual time of five in the morning. If I get up early, I can
comb my hair and shower without having to compete with anyone
else. Dressing in a crowd increases my anxiety. I am shaky, and I
take deep breaths to try to calm the tension that engulfs me. Paul
Harder, the administrator of the school, notices that I am up early
again and alone in the hallway. He approaches me.

"How are things going?"

It is the invitation that I need, and I soon spill out my lone-
liness, my anxiety, and my unhappiness with life as it is at home.
Just talking to someone is calming, and he says the words to me
that I will hear several times over in the next few years and that
eventually allow me to release myself from my father's psychological prison.

"You are an adult, and God does not require you to stay under
your father's roof."

That is a freeing thought to me, but my brain counters with,
but you don't understand. It's not that easy.

Another week has passed at Bible school, and I am beginning
to feel at home. I have even started sleeping through the night.
There are classes to attend during the day and various assigned
chores each evening. I especially enjoy the games in the evening

and have tried my hand at volleyball, basketball, Ping-Pong, and shuffleboard. I have started to joke with the other young people, and slowly I feel my reserve lessening. I have developed an attraction to one of the young men, and out of it has grown a secret hope that he might be interested in me also. That spark of infatuation adds a new zest to life that I have not experienced for quite some time. As I emerge from my shell, I begin to make connections with some of the other girls in my dorm. A deep friendship develops with one young lady, Rebecca Bontrager, who also happens to have agreed to be the local Mennonite schoolteacher this coming year. That means that she will still be around after the rest of the students go back to their homes in faraway places.

The last week passes all too fast, and before I know it, I am home in my bedroom unpacking my suitcases. I have no desire to return to the barn. *I don't know how I am going to adjust to home again. Bible school provided a sense of camaraderie, laughter, and a chance to get closer to Jesus without feeling judged. Oh Lord, give me the strength to serve you and to trust that you will work something out so that I can be freed from my obligation to the farm.*

From a farming perspective, the summer of 1979 is no different from any other. There are always tensions at home, but I am further distressed by the tensions that have also developed at church. Church used to be my refuge from the daily grind, and, now that I have made a friend at Bible school, I was looking forward to that friendly connection every Sunday. But Daddy and Mama view the Mennonite fellowship group in a different light since the visit of the two ministers. They feel it is time to speak their mind on the "sinful" practices going on at church. It has been the traditional practice of most conservative Mennonite churches for the men and women to sit on opposite sides of the church. Some of the more progressive churches, such as Moorland, have begun, instead, to sit together as families on one bench. Daddy and Mama have always been opposed to this new practice.

"The only right way is for the women to sit on one side of the church and the men on the other. Husbands and wives are touching each other during the church service, and this leads to thoughts about things other than God."

Daddy and Mama now take every opportunity during the weekly Sunday school discussions to interject into the lesson how sinful this practice is. I just want to disappear. I am torn between loyalty to my parents and just wanting to be accepted somewhere. And at home, Daddy, Mama, and Paul continue to go to pipeline meetings every week or two throughout the summer. The opposition group is making significant progress in blocking the proposed pipeline, and Daddy feels that his continued participation is justified regardless of what the church's position is.

Dawn is just beginning its spread over the horizon as I step out of the milk-house door on this mid-September day. As I glance toward the east, another silo stands silhouetted against the first rays of day. It has risen from its foundation in the last week to take its place on the landscape by the newer section of free-stall barn. It will not have long to wait to be filled with freshly cut silage for the feeding of the additional cows this winter.

But silos are not my interest today. I must hurry if I am going to get washed up and changed before the group of Mennonite young people from Moorland come by to pick me up at six. Rebecca, my friend, called me last evening and asked if I wanted to go along with the group to the Twin Cities. I hesitated. Right now, I would really just prefer to hide from the world, but it did sound like fun—and, even more amazingly, Daddy said yes. I jumped out of bed early in order to get as much of the milking done as possible. Daddy and the boys still need to finish up, but at least I did my part.

I listen to the happy chatter around me as we cruise toward the zoo in Minnesota's biggest city. I start to relax and allow myself to feel the excitement of the day. Rebecca and I catch up on the events of the past few weeks. She has just returned from Iowa to begin another year of teaching at the small church school at Moorland. Before I know it, we are at our destination, and the day flies by as we meander through the various displays. It is a game of searching for animals that really aren't too concerned with being found. Giraffes have a hard time hiding, though, and I find their gracefulness amazing.

After lunch, the suggestion is made that we should try to catch one of the paddleboats that make daily excursions up and down the Mississippi River. Now, that sounds like fun. I have always been enthralled by boats. It is a warm day for September, and autumn is just starting to paint the trees along the shoreline with blazing reds and yellows. I stand on the upper deck as the breeze blows through my hair and take in the beauty of the fall day. The river stretches away into the distance. I am glad that I came. *If life could only be this peaceful every day.* The sun is low in the western sky when we again dock.

Chatter swirls around me on the way home, and I feel connected again in some small way to this group of people.

It has been only a week since the fun trip to the cities. Tonight, Saul Schowalter, the bishop, called during supper to say that the ministers are coming again tomorrow evening to talk. My stomach muscles tighten, and I find myself taking short, shallow breaths. That sick feeling in my stomach rises up into my throat and threatens to choke me.

Right at seven o'clock the next evening, the men are ushered into our dining/living room. Both men are clean-shaven and neatly dressed in long-sleeved shirts and dress pants. They are offered kitchen table chairs upon which to be seated. I curl into the recliner in the corner and quietly listen to the conversation. It has been almost a year since the ministers initially approached Daddy with their concerns over his involvement with the pipeline protest group. They are aware that he has continued with his involvement. I can see by the firm set of Daddy's jaw and his fixed, unsmiling countenance that he has no intention of admitting any wrongdoing. He reiterates that he has done nothing wrong and that his heart does not condemn him. Mama tries to divert the discussion in another direction by bringing to the attention of the ministers the numerous ways she feels that they themselves are not following the Bible's teachings by the way they do things. In the light of Daddy and Mama's response, we are informed that no one in our family will be served communion until Daddy is willing to humbly admit that he has transgressed the principles of the Mennonite church and publicly ask for forgiveness. *Like that is ever going to happen. I have never heard Daddy admit that he is wrong in any situation.*

Sunday dawns cloudy. The dark clouds do not help my mood any. Daddy and Mama have taken Rebecca home to Iowa for the day, so Paul, Joseph, and I go to church by ourselves. Today is communion Sunday, but we cannot participate. The sacrament of communion in the Mennonite church is observed only two times per year, and it is served only to those members who profess to be in good standing with God and the church. *Why did we come here*

today? I feel like a terrible sinner, and all the tears in the world cannot
wash away the shame of the family I belong to.

I struggle to open my eyes as I come to the realization that the alarm is sending out its usual four-in-the-morning shrill call. Weariness envelopes me, but I know I need to get up if there is any chance that we will get to church today. I had just gotten back in bed at two, after feeding two newborn calves during the night. I didn't get to bed initially until well after ten o'clock last evening. A calf was born during the late evening, and I had to make sure it got its first colostrum. Then I needed to clean up the pen and switch animals around before turning in. I wanted the most likely of the remaining three expectant first-time mamas to have the clean bedded pen for her baby. Having only one calving pen makes it extremely difficult when several cows calve in the same day. But there is nothing I can do about it.

"We just have to make the best of it," is Daddy's response.

If all three calve tonight, the other two will have to give birth tied in the sickroom stalls. I bedded them down the best that I could and then headed for bed; setting the alarm for one o'clock so that I might check on things. My journey to the barn during the night revealed one calf flopping around the room on the wet, slippery floor and the one in the pen needing some pulling assistance. I grab the silver calf-puller chains with handles, slip the loops around the protruding legs, and do my "sit on the floor, prop my feet on the back of the cow, and pull" thing. Soon there is another sloppy calf shaking its slicked-down head and rocking back and forth as it tries to get adjusted to this new world. As a young child, I used to sit for hours and wait to watch this wonder of birth. Now, it has become just one more repeating, exhausting activity in my life. I am tired and not in the mood to milk two heifers by hand in the middle of the night. Instead, I heat some of the reserve frozen colostrum that we have saved and feed both babies. I will replace the reserve in the morning, once we get these two milked the modern way. By the time I get everyone resituated, an hour has passed. I head back to the house to crash back into bed.

I make my way to the sickroom just off the parlor as my first order of business. I sigh with relief. There are no new calves to care for before I begin the milking chores. My relief is short-lived, though, when Joseph comes back from getting the cows around for milking. He has bad news. There is a new calf out in the free-stall barn. My heart sinks. *No! This is not what I need right now.* I evidently missed the signs of impending labor on one cow. Having the calf born out in the dirty, manure-coated barn distresses me greatly. Not only is it a reflection on my herdsman skills, but the calves usually don't do nearly as well, due to being exposed to all that filth at their most vulnerable time of life. Joseph gathers up the calf and brings it into the sickroom. He cleans it up the best that he can while I get the milking underway. By the time we are nearing the end of milking, one more calf has made its entrance into the world in the calving pen. I am feeling overwhelmed. I think this is a record. We have had five new babies in less than twelve hours. *Is there no end to all these calves?*

In spite of all the potential for things turning into a disaster on this Sunday morning, everything falls together fairly well. We slip into our pews only a few minutes late. I would have been very upset if we hadn't made it to church today because this day, December 30, 1979, is the first day of the new Bible school session for the coming year. Neither Joseph nor I will be attending Bible school this year, but I am looking forward to the added social interaction and contacts that will be available on Sundays for the next three months.

White flakes cascade from the sky as I make my way to the barn. *No!* This is April. Rebecca and I are supposed to leave for her home in Iowa today. She has asked me to come home with her over the Easter holidays, and I was so looking forward to this trip. Her church host family brought her last evening, so at least I don't need to think about going to pick her up too. *Maybe it will stop snowing by the time I am done with the chores.* But by mid-morning when we are ready to leave, snow is still falling heavily. Several inches have accumulated. I am worried but we decide to "go for it." I strain my eyes to pick out the road as we crawl at forty miles per hour through the eerie expanse of whiteness. As we slowly make our way south, the precipitation lessens and becomes big plops on the windshield. Then it is raining. As I relax, my head begins to nod. Rebecca takes over the driving, and I allow sleep to overtake me. Before I know it, we are rolling into the driveway of Rebecca's parents' home.

I like this getting up after the sun is already shining. Breakfast is served and then the family gathers for devotions. Yesterday, we went to the closest city in the morning to pass out gospel tracts, then stopped at a restaurant afterward to eat. Eating out is not something our family does. Daddy and Mama always consider it to be an extravagant and unnecessary expense. I didn't want to admit I had no idea what I was doing, so I just watched Rebecca so as not to make a fool of myself. Later, we returned to the family home to play games.

This morning, Rebecca mentions that the young people are having a volleyball game and then later, we will go shopping together. I am fascinated by the different lives that other people seem to live. I find myself pulled between wanting to try more new and different things and returning to the old predictable secure routine of just getting up and working from morning until night.

The clock hands already push toward seven before any signs of life reach my ears on this Easter Sunday. I have been awake for more than an hour already. I sit and chat with my friend while she makes breakfast for her family.

"We're having communion today," Rebecca shares.

A thought crosses my mind. "Really?" I respond, "Do you think I can take communion here?"

She and I agree that I haven't done anything wrong, and nobody here knows anything about the recent problems between my folks and the church at home. I make my decision. When the minister comes around to serve each member a piece of the bread and a sip from the cup at the end of the service, I stand to accept my portion along with everyone else. A renewed commitment to live my faith fills my heart, and my soul feels cleansed.

After the service, we eat another family dinner at Rebecca's home and then it is time to head back. I have really enjoyed the weekend, and I am not looking forward to returning to the life that is mine. I struggle to push back the depression that threatens to engulf me as we head north toward home.

It is hot for the first day of May. The corn planter is hooked to the 4430 and sits poised to begin the yearly task of placing the seeds in the soil. For the last week, I have been working ground between milkings, preparing the land for another crop year. This morning, Joseph and I got the morning milking done a little earlier than usual and Daddy has asked me to go town to get a load of seed corn from the Dekalb dealer. I love these off-farm trips, as they give me a sense of importance and freedom. The thirty-minute drive allows the fresh spring air to blow through the open pickup window and gives my spirits a lift. This time of year always renews my hope that maybe this year will be a better one. It takes only a short time to heave twenty-five bags of seed corn into the truck bed. Within another thirty minutes, I am back home, hoisting the bags and emptying them into the planter.

As we close the lids on the planter boxes, the Germania Dairy equipment installation crew boss approaches Daddy. He tells him that he is missing some key parts for installing the new milking equipment. I jump at the chance to make another trip to town for the needed items. We cannot milk tonight until the job is done, so getting the parts is a priority. And it gives me a chance to make another solo trip to town.

Daddy has been looking at and talking about buying automatic take-off milking machines for quite some time. Over the last week, the workmen have been installing bits and pieces. Today will be the final changeover to the new setup. I am excited. Since I spend a huge amount of time milking alone, this should make my job easier. I will take any help that I can get. I would much prefer to milk fewer cows, but since my pleas for that go unheard, I am more than willing to make this elite, expensive purchase my partner.

I really want to watch the installation but it is too nice of a day to "waste." After my return from town, I swing up into the four-wheel-drive tractor and head for the field with the digger. I can see the corn planter in the distance, making its way up and down the neighboring field. For the next three hours, the black soil smooths into wavy lines behind me. My eyes soon grow heavy from the rocking motion of the tractor and the ceaseless, unvarying roar of the engine. I allow myself the luxury of dozing intermittently. After all, there is nothing to hit and there are no prizes for driving straight.

As the sun begins its western descent, it is time to think about milking. I park the tractor by the machine shed and walk toward the barn. Opening the milk-house door, I can see tools and equipment strewn everywhere. The sound of hammering reaches my ears.

"Are you going to be ready any time soon?" I ask.

"It's going to be several hours yet before we will have things far enough along for you to milk tonight," Is the reply I receive.

Just great! I decide to hang out and help clean up the best that I can. Maybe my help will speed up the process.

The cows are becoming impatient with the humans and want to be milked. The bawling begins. It increases in volume and frequency until constant mooing assaults our ears. By seven thirty, when we are finally ready to begin, the cows are more than ready to rush the parlor. They fight and push to get in the doors. I cut off the surging mob and slam the door after six animals have entered on each side. I wash and dry each udder, then attach the new machines to the six animals on the east side of the parlor before moving on to the second side. It is hard to ignore the first side and just let these "smart" machines decide when those animals are fully milked. My instinct is to go back and check on things, but I force myself to move on. Before I have the next row prepped and the milking machines on them, I can hear the flop of the cups and the tinkle of the metal clicking against the piping as the finished machines disconnect. *Wow! This is quite the concept.* But we have started four hours late tonight, so it is midnight before I finally fall into bed, exhausted, on this first day of a new way of milking.

The next morning, I discover the primary benefit of having milking machines that take themselves off. Weariness from only four hours of sleep overwhelms me, and I lean on the milk receiver jar while I wait for the last machines to detach. My eyes drift shut, and the world disappears into background noise. *This works pretty well.* I just need to wake up every once in a while to get more cows in and prepped and then I can go back to my napping. Needless to say, it takes me just as long or longer to milk than before, but I think I have mastered the skill of working while sleeping.

Mooooo! Moooo! The persistent bawling of a seemingly dis-tressed animal reaches my ears as I make my way to the barn. I open the door leading to the free-stall barn and climb up onto my view perch. *That's funny. I keep hearing this bawling but it sounds far away, and it keeps moving around.* I can't see any animal that seems to be making the noise, so I return to the parlor to get ready for the evening milking. Soon, Joseph makes his way into the parlor from getting the first group of cows into the holding area.

"There was a manure pit cover half off on the other side of the barn," he reports. "All the animals were going around the hole, so I don't think any cows fell in."

We both hope that that is the case, because having a cow down in the manure pit would be a nightmare. Paul stirred and pumped the pit last week, before the last crop was planted. One of the covers must not have gotten put back on just right. Not want-ing to even think that a cow might have fallen in, we continue with the evening milking. As I herd the last members of the first group of cows into the parlor, I realize that we are short one cow. We can no longer deny the obvious; the continuing bawling, the manure pit cover kicked to the side, and the missing cow all fit to-gether. My heart sinks. I send Joseph in search of Daddy and Paul.

We all gather around the pit opening as Paul leans in with

the flashlight. The light is reflected back at us from two shining eyes. A black cow wanders around in three feet of black manure in the dark, approximately 40-foot-by-100-foot under-barn pit.

One of the dangers of unventilated manure pits is the presence of methane gas. More than one person has died from entering a pit due to the gas. Apparently, the methane gas level is not too high in there right now, or the cow would be dead. But going into the pit without oxygen would still be foolhardy. Therefore, Daddy has gone to the fire department in the closest town eight miles away and borrowed two oxygen tanks. Paul and Joseph both pull on hip boots, then each straps on an oxygen tank and mask. I can feel my stomach muscles ball into a knot as they descend the ladder into the pit. I don't even want to think about what the end result of this could be. Walking around in this foul dungeon, chasing after a cow who keeps moving, would not be my idea of fun for any day. Not only is the gas a concern, but a person could drown if he stumbled and fell into the thigh-deep liquid. As for my brothers, trying to trap and rope the animal in this vast sea of foul waste proves to be futile. They trail around and around after the wandering animal. Finally, a decision is made to guide the animal toward the opening and to have Daddy try to catch her with a rope from above. After several tries, this proves to be successful.

I hold my breath as Daddy hooks the rope onto the backhoe bucket. I am horrified. The only way to get the cow back up is to lift her straight up through the four-foot-by-three-foot hole using a rope tied around her neck. Joseph has been left in the pit to try to calm the animal until the lift begins. We have no more than three or four minutes to get this task completed if we do not wish to have a dead cow, by hanging, on our hands.

"Go! Go!" shouts Daddy to Paul on the backhoe tractor seat as the cow's bugged-out eyes appear through the hole. The tractor lurches forward, dragging the struggling animal with it. I realize my legs are shaking and my breath is coming in gasps, but our rescued cow looks none the worse from her ordeal. She catches her breath and then springs to her feet.

It is midnight again before we fall into bed, but I am unable to sleep. I lie there thinking about this fiasco. I always find it interesting that Paul receives hardly a reprimand, while Joseph would have been thoroughly shamed and chastised if he had been the one responsible for this mess.

Little rain has fallen in April and May, making for a smooth planting season. However, the area farmers were beginning to worry about the lack of rain. Then, last evening, the western sky began to darken around eight o'clock. It soon took on a strange gray hue. Daddy turned on the radio just in time to hear reports of ninety- to one-hundred-mile-per-hour winds with rain and golf-ball-sized hail about twenty-five miles west of the farm. The storm was headed our way. The wind had begun to pick up by the time Paul and Joseph dashed out to shut doors and secure everything as much as possible. They arrived back in the house just in time for all of us to hurry to the basement. The wind howled, and the rain lashed against the siding. And then we were engulfed in darkness as the power went out. Throughout the night, thunderstorm followed thunderstorm, making it difficult to sleep. By morning, we had received more than five inches of rain. The corn and soybeans had been shredded by the wind-driven rain, and the plants looked rather sick.

During the following week, we are drenched with two more heavy rainstorms. The total rainfall is more than ten inches. Then a fourth storm on June 19 drops the dreaded hail—the size of tennis balls. As the ice balls pound the ground, they cut and shred the tender shoots of corn and emerging soybean plants. In the house, the sound of breaking glass, coming from the direction of the kitchen, reaches our ears. We cringe when the same sound explodes from the western living room window. Once the deluge has stopped, Daddy surveys the damage.

"One third of the corn has been totally cut off, and the rest is all shredded," he reports. "I hope that there will at least be enough corn to fill the silos in the fall."

A week later, the heat begins. Each day of this week in mid-July, the thermometer has touched one hundred degrees by mid-afternoon. The sweat pours off my forehead when I am just sitting in the house. I dread going to the barn to milk. The cows stand with their mouths hanging open, panting. Milk production has dropped way off. But I have come up with a daily ritual that makes the heat in the parlor at least tolerable. My shoes are left in the milk house. My bare feet slap against the cool, wet concrete of the parlor floor as I pad around the pit. I just have to remember to keep my toes out from under sharp hooves if I need to leave the pit to chase a wayward cow. My other trick is to trickle water down the back of my dress with the water hose. As my clothes dry, I repeat the process. Ah. It feels delicious to have that cold trace down my back. We have no air conditioning in the house, so sleeping is miserable. We are all becoming thoroughly irritable.

Maybe it is the heat or maybe it is just life, but I am becoming increasingly more discouraged and angry as the summer wears on. I feel like my life is controlled by what Daddy wants, and I am powerless to do anything about it. I am twenty-two years old, but I might just as well be sixteen. There is no time for me to do anything that I would like to do. Not only that, but Daddy doesn't even try to understand how I feel. A conversation with Daddy is one-sided; he talks at me, and I am supposed to listen. Most of the time, I am able to keep my feelings to myself until that proverbial "straw that breaks the camel's back" is added and then I explode into hateful words.

"Will you buy me a tape recorder and player?" I ask Mama this evening at supper. "I want to buy some tapes to listen to music in my room before I go to sleep."

"We don't have any money for things like that," Daddy interjects.

I can feel the heat rising in my face, and the words are out before I think.

"I can't do anything around here but work. You have money for all the projects you want to do on the farm, but heaven forbid that you would spend any money on us."

I can see the lines in Daddy's face tighten, and his jaw sets as he glares at me. I get up and disappear to my bedroom before the "sermon" can begin. I bury my face in my pillow and sob my heart out. Hopelessness descends over me like a suffocating cloud. For the next two days, I force myself to go about my work. I have no desire to do anything.

A couple of weeks later, on July 23, I am leafing through the local *Advertiser* when I notice an ad that says "Emergency Medical Technicians wanted for ambulance service. Class starts on September 15." My attention is grabbed. I know that I want to do this. But do I dare even entertain such a thought?

In spite of the nagging voice in my head that tells me this is never going to work, I pick up the phone the next day when no one is around and dial the number listed in the ad. My heart pounds, and I hold my breath as I wait for the persistent ringing to be answered. I hear the click of the answering machine as it kicks in, and I let my breath out slowly. I am both disappointed and relieved that I don't have to try to talk to a real person. I leave my name and phone number and quickly hang up. *What was I thinking?*

Two weeks pass before I get a return call from the director of the ambulance service. I have pretty much convinced myself by now that it would never be allowed anyway. As I listen to the caller, though, the desire in my heart is revived. The class is on Monday evenings from six to ten. The director invites me to come to the ambulance picnic on August 11 and meet the crew. If I decide to join the class, I can sign the papers then. I do not know what to say. *How can I ever make this work?* But I really want to do this, and one day a week doesn't seem like that big of a deal. I milk early on picnic day and sneak away, leaving Joseph to finish up. Then I do an irrational thing. I sign up for the class.

September 15 dawns cloudy and cool. I try to go about my usual work for the day, but I am apprehensive and tense. Daddy is giving me the silent treatment. I decided to finally tell him a couple of days ago that I had signed up for this class. I did not ask his permission.

"How do you think we are going to get the harvest done when you go running off? This is not the time of year to be doing this," he lectures.

Ignoring his objections, I milk early and head for town, eight miles away. I find the class interesting and exciting, but there does seem to be a lot of studying. *How am I ever going to get all this studying done and still keep Daddy happy?*

Throughout the next week, I grab every free minute to study. Daddy and Paul are building another grain bin, our fourth, and one of my days goes into helping to build the bin. I do not dare mention my need to study. The work always comes first. I come home from my second class on the following Monday evening to a furious father.

"This is ridiculous. Your place is at home, here, helping to make a go of the farm. I expect that you will be available to run the dryer during corn harvest."

Tension fills my body over the next two days as I struggle to decide if I will follow my heart or give in to my father's wishes. I am sick to my stomach and just pick at my food. I find myself shaking and unable to sleep. Finally, the tears come spilling out as I milk alone in the parlor the next evening. Despair and anger fill my soul, and I allow the sobs to go on and on.

The next evening is an extra class on Cardiopulmonary Resuscitation (CPR) that is mandatory. My stomach stays tied in a knot all day as I go about my work. As quietly as possible, I disappear down the lane just before six. Daddy and Paul have been pouring cement all day for the new truck scale that they have installed. Once that is done, they will be ready to start the corn harvest. When I return around ten, I am again met by a stern, livid father who now forbids me to milk early anymore.

"It messes up the cows' routine, which lowers milk production," he insists.

I have had all I can take. I am fuming, but I feel like I have no choice but to call the ambulance director the next morning and drop out of the class. I don't know how else to release this pressure that is consuming me. I am disgusted with my father and ashamed of myself. A deep, dark cloud descends over me. Another dream has been killed. I pray to God that he will somehow change my father or my situation, as I don't know how much longer I can take this. Two weeks later, on my twenty-third birthday, I drive to town to pay off the money that I owe for the class; money that I wouldn't have had to pay if I had completed it—money that I had to take out of my small savings account.

Relationships at the Moorland Mennonite church remain strained between Daddy and Mama and others in attendance there. I cringe at the critical and cutting words Daddy and Mama speak during discussions. I am both appalled and ashamed. The fall date for communion comes and goes on October 12 with all of us still being denied participation. This seems to be the turning point for Daddy and Mama, as they make a decision that we are not going to attend church where we are treated this way. Alternatively, we begin attending non-Mennonite churches on some Sundays and no church on other Sundays.

I cannot overcome the censure that rests on the whole family, so I tell myself that it really doesn't matter much to me anyway what we do. I no longer have a close friend at church either, as Rebecca is not teaching at the church school this year. She has become engaged to a young man that she has been dating for some time and is moving on with her life. The wedding has been set for December 13. I am happy for Rebecca, but a part of me feels left behind while life for others moves on.

I rip open the letter with Rebecca's return address and read the words she has written. I am amazed and thrilled. She is not only inviting me to her wedding but asking me to be the gift opener at the reception. I have never before been asked to be a part of anyone's wedding, and I feel honored. That means I have a couple of months to buy the material and make the dress that I will wear. A new excitement infuses my spirit, and I head for my sewing machine during any spare moments.

The alarm is sending out its annoying beeping at the usual dark hour of 4:00 a.m. I moan as I reach out to silence it. Then I remember. *Today's the day!* It is Rebecca's wedding day. I hurriedly pull on my clothes and clatter down the stairs. Paul and Joseph will be doing the milking today while Daddy drives me to the wedding. Letting me drive alone this far is not something Daddy will allow.

The miles roll away under the tires as the sky slowly brightens to the east. The sun is just peeking over the horizon as we pull into the church parking lot in Iowa. The church is abuzz with activity. Relatives of both families and members of the church community are busy getting the food ready. Rebecca gives me a huge hug when she sees me. She wastes no time in pulling me into the activity. I am shown to a table in the dining area where I will take the gifts that the guests come bearing. Then I will unwrap them for all to see.

Before I know it, I find myself filing into the pew at the back of the church with the other young people who are serving at the reception. The peach-colored cape dresses that the young ladies wear stand out in stark contrast to the dark-colored, plain suits of the young men. There are no fancy clothes at Mennonite weddings. The bride wears the traditional white dress. The groom gets to wear a new suit if he wants, but the dress and the suit are simple and in the traditional style of everyday dress. A wedding is a solemn time of commitment for the two exchanging vows but also a time of celebration for family and friends. Food, lots of it, is the primary focus at the reception, to facilitate sharing together. There will be no dance, and no alcohol will be served.

I unwrap and organize the gifts while the buzz of voices bounces around me. I am happy just to absorb the cheerfulness that the crowd exudes. I don't really know a lot of people here, but I feel welcome and included. It is a great day.

Two weeks have passed since the wedding, and the winter term of Bible school starts tomorrow. I always look forward to the different speakers and the many young people that are present at Sunday services during the twelve weeks that Bible school is in session. In spite of our strained connection with the local congregation, I think there is an unspoken understanding in our family that we will make a concerted effort to attend services at the school during these three months of the year when other ministers are present.

This morning, Paul Harder, the school administrator, called.

"Would you be willing to teach the young women's Sunday school class tomorrow?" he asks.

My breath catches. *No. I cannot do that. I am not a teacher, and I have no desire to stand in front of anyone. Mostly though, I am ashamed of who I am, and I do not feel I have any spiritual insights to share with other young people.* I tell him, "No."

When I hang up, Mama turns to me. "What's the matter with you? It's an honor to teach Sunday school. You call him back and tell him you will do it."

I look at her, stunned.

"No, I am not going to," I respond.

So Mama picks up the telephone, calls Paul and tells him that she herself will teach the Sunday school class. I am humiliated, and I am hurt by her insensitivity to the position they have placed me in by their superior attitude toward anything to do with the church. I go to my room and cry.

I am still feeling alienated from everyone as we slide into

our seats in the chapel the next day, but as I look around at the new students who have come for this term, my heart skips a beat, and there is a catch in my breath. I notice Wesley Dyck seated among the young men. Though he possesses no outstanding facial features, his smile more than makes up for his short frame and non-attention-grabbing normalness. Wes is the same young man that I had found myself attracted to while attending Bible school a couple of years ago. His humor and his openness were refreshing to my spirit. Excitement creeps in as I allow my mind to wander during the service. Maybe, just maybe, there is hope yet for something more than a friendship to develop. After the service, our family stays for dinner at the school, and I am able to discreetly approach Wesley. We laugh and joke as we reconnect. And before I leave with my folks for the day, I have secured a yes from Wes and three other young people to come to our house for dinner the next Sunday.

The six weeks that Wesley is in the community go by way too fast. A heart-pounding energy fills me during the week, and my spirit is light. Wes and I talk and laugh after church as I mingle with the other young people. But beyond presenting me with his autographed picture inscribed with encouraging words on his last day, February 22, there does not seem to be any interest on his part in making the relationship anything more than a friendship. With disappointment, I realize that I need to let go of my fantasies as he drives away back to his own life. A new realization is also beginning to dawn as I watch other young people connect, develop relationships, and move on toward marriage. I have always subconsciously known that the standing of one's parents in an Anabaptist community is an unwritten standard against which to judge the acceptability of one's prospective partner. Therefore, the reputation of my father and our family in this close-knit Mennonite community is creating a huge stumbling block for me in this regard. No decent Mennonite young man is going to seriously consider any kind of a romantic relationship with me.

The sound of a slamming car door reaches my ears. I glance out the house window to see Daddy and Joseph walking toward the house. Joseph trails behind Daddy, and the droop of his head, along with the slump of his shoulders, tells me all that I need to know. He has flunked a fourth time. Just over a year ago, Daddy finally agreed to allow Joseph, at age twenty-one, to get a driver's license permit. But he has not allowed him to practice driving.

"He's not going to drive any of my vehicles. He's too careless with everything."

"And how is he supposed to learn to drive?" I ask.

"He thinks he's so smart. He'll have to figure it out on his own." was the response I received.

Now, Joseph has been going every week for the last four weeks in an effort to pass the behind-the-wheel driver's license exam before the permit expires. As we begin our dinner, Daddy laughs and tells everyone that Joseph has flunked again.

"You're not so smart after all, are you? You thought you could show up the cop, and he showed you."

Joe does not respond but stares straight ahead, avoiding any eye contact. My heart goes out to him. I too can feel the old, familiar anger begin to creep outward from deep in my soul and further erode what little respect I have left for my father. In fact, Paul, Joseph, and I no longer call this man Daddy in our everyday conversation. Among the three of us, we have come to refer to him as Pappy. Pappy is a term that has sprung up in conversation among some Mennonite teenagers when referring to their parents. Daddy has vehemently declared to us that this term is disrespectful of one's parents and that if those teenagers were his, he would put a stop to its use. To us, disrespect is what our father deserves at this point, but because openly defying him would be disastrous, we have created our own silent defiance. To his face, we simply don't address him with any title. I glance across the table at my grinning father and wonder what he is going to say when he finds out that I have talked to a minister at the Bible school, asking for help with our whole situation. The last two days, I have been physically sick from being worried to death about how he is going to react.

It seems that anger followed by depression has become my constant companion in the past weeks, and it does not take very much to trigger it. Last week was when I finally made this decision to ask for help from one of the ministers at the Bible school. I went along with Mama to the dentist, and, while she was getting her teeth done, I went "shopping." With my stomach tied in a knot and tension wrapping its bands around my heart, I drove to the Bible school. I asked to speak with Harold Ewert, the current administrator. My despair over having no choice of my own came spilling out. Brother Harold agreed to talk to Pappy and try to get him to change his approach to us. But as I drove away, I was beginning to have second thoughts. *I hope this wasn't a mistake. Oh God! Help me!*

Over the course of the last three days, I have fallen into a deep depression and can hardly function from the fear and hopelessness that fills me. It takes all my effort just to drag myself through the week. *I wish I had just kept quiet.*

Tonight, as we sit down at the supper table, I can see that Pappy is upset. A strained silence reigns for most of the meal. I pull out the book that I keep close to the table for such purposes and read while I pick at my food, to distract myself from the rising tension. Then Pappy clears his throat.

"It is none of anybody's business what we do here at home. I can't believe that my children are willing to betray me by telling other people our business. I've done all this for you and this is the thanks I get."

And then he begins to sob, as if I have committed the most terrible offense. I am disgusted by his use of tears to further manipulate us and by his unwillingness to admit that we, as a family, have a problem. Mama begins to cry as well. I take my book and escape from the table. I feel the beginning of the stabbing pain in my stomach and nausea wells up.

The spring of 1981 came early. Corn planting began in late April, and all the seeds lay germinating in the soil by the fifteenth of May. Then it was time to turn our thoughts to the building of another barn. Yes, another barn. This barn will have pens for the young heifers on one side and a place for hay storage on the other. The hauling of loads of sand and gravel occupies Paul's and my days for a week. We get our old farm trucks loaded at the gravel pit by the town just nine miles southwest of the farm and dump the fill just behind the old barn.

Soon after this, Pappy does an unexpected thing. He hires an area man to help some with the field work, but his primary responsibility is to help with the milking. Maybe my asking for someone to talk to him has had some effect after all. Maybe, just maybe, if we have some hired help, I can think about pursuing my dreams of going to school.

The first group of cows is already packed into the holding area, and I am putting the first milking machines on when the milk-house door opens and Brian appears.

"Hi sweetheart" is his greeting.

I smile. "Hello."

Brian has been employed for almost a month. I do appreciate his help with the milking, but sometimes I think my life has gotten more stressful with his presence rather than less. Once both rows of milkers are on, I lean against the milk receiver jar to wait for the machines to finish. Brian approaches, puts an arm on both sides of me, and presses his body against mine.

"Are you ready to go romp in the hay? We could have a grand old time," he teases. I don't really know how to take him, but I give a short laugh and push him away. He's a married man, and I don't really believe he is serious. At least, I didn't at first; now I am not so sure.

"No, we would just get caught," I jest in return.

"How about a kiss then, for a lonely man?" he intones.

I shake my head. "I don't think so."

This kind of sexual innuendo has been going on since the first week. It is beginning to stir up feelings in me that I did not even know I had. I do not have a good enough relationship with Pappy anymore that I would even consider sharing this situation with him. A part of me knows that if this venture into hiring someone goes bad, Pappy will just say that it was a dumb idea in the first place. And at this point, having someone to take my place is of paramount importance in my mind if I am ever going to be able to make a different life for myself. I have tried to just tell Brian that I am not interested, but my words are pretty much ignored and his "teasing" is relentless—to the point that I have come to believe that he is pushing to see exactly how far I will go. And though I had once thought I knew how far I would go, now I am becoming mightily confused.

In the last month, I have also secretly taken one more step in the direction of moving ahead with my dreams. I have sent for and received information in the mail on the programs available through two separate technical colleges in the area. I pore over the brochures in the afternoons trying to figure out if there is any way I can juggle going to school and performing my duties on the farm. I have also made a decision that I want to go to Bible school next winter at Emanuel Bible School in Ash Hill, Ohio. I want to get far away, just for a little while. Though I have no idea how I am going to begin to make any of my dreams come true, thinking and planning, even if the chances of it happening are slim, give me the small hope I need to keep getting out of bed each day.

The summer has slid into July. It is muggy and warm. Just a day ago, lightning flashed and thunder rumbled and the rain came cascading down during the night. One of the thunder rumbles rolled on longer than normal. It shook the whole house. But thinking it was only the storm, we all groggily returned to sleep. After Joseph and I had gone to the barn in the morning, Paul detoured to check the rain gauge on his way out. Five inches of water sat in the tapered tube. Turning from the rain gauge, he was shocked to find himself facing a gaping hole in the east side of the basement wall. The side of the house hung suspended in space; held up by the one continuous beam across that section. Bricks and soupy mud covered the basement floor. The heavy rain had caused the wall of the basement to fail leaving the physical security of our home, like the emotional security of the rest of my life, ready to collapse.

Just a morning later, I put the milking equipment together myself and flip the switch to start the pump. Brian is usually here to help by now. *Maybe he will be here soon.* I sigh. This is the third time that he has been late in the last couple of weeks. I struggle with the milking alone. Later, Pappy strides through the parlor on his way to feed the cows.

"Brian called to say his wife is not feeling well. He won't be coming today," he begins then he grumbles, "Just what we need, an undependable hired man."

I try to hold my feelings of abandonment and anger at bay. I just need to get through the milking. Then I can move on to the project that I am eagerly looking forward to today during what hours of free time that I have. I have bought material and started sewing new dresses in preparation for going away to Bible school next winter. In fact, the application to attend is in the envelope and ready for mailing today. It will be a perfect day for secretly mailing something, as everyone will be gone.

After breakfast, the menfolk head north, with the trucks, to a farm about fifteen miles away where they are tearing down a used silo. This silo will be re-erected before fall by the newer free-stall barn, alongside the other silo already there. Before it can be put back up though, the mortar needs to be chipped from the staves so that new mortar can be applied. Joseph is assigned this tedious job that will keep him busy for the next month or so.

"And when you get that project done," Pappy says to Joseph, "you can break up those rocks behind the barn with the sledge-hammer. We might as well use them in the cow yard before we cement that."

The building of new farm structures seems to be constant. I do not understand this need to keep expanding and building. In fact, I am overwhelmed by it. There simply is no time for life. I have tried more than once to talk to Pappy about cutting back so that we have time to enjoy life, but I might just as well talk to a stone wall. "Idleness is the devil's workshop." and "Work never hurt anyone." These are some of his favorite sayings. And he seems determined to make sure that Joseph definitely experiences this conviction of his. Why Joseph takes the brunt, I do not know or understand.

A week later, I stand chatting with the veterinarian by his truck. He is scrubbing his boots and putting away his equipment after treating a sick cow. I look up to see a sheriff's car stop and the deputy get out. A few minutes later, Brian gets in his pickup, and the dirt flies as he speeds away. *What is going on?* Ever since that day last week that he did not come to work because his wife "was not feeling well," Brian has been acting strangely. He has been withdrawn into his own little world, sullen and agitated.

"What's wrong?" I tried to draw him out.

"Nothing." He shrugged and turned away. "My wife is just having some back problems."

I did not believe him. I suspected that something else was going on. Today, Brian does not return for the evening milking after his strange departure.

The day following the sheriff's visit, Brian again does not show up for work. This morning, he walks in late. He avoids my gaze and goes about washing and wiping the cows' udders without saying a word. We milk in silence for a while, but I am curious, and I start to rib him about the sheriff coming to see him. He erupts in anger.

"It's none of your business. I'm done here."

He turns and stomps out of the parlor, banging the door behind him. I am stunned. A part of me is relieved that he is gone, but the bigger part of me is devastated and panicked. *How am I ever going to go to college or even Bible school without extra help on the farm?* Pappy had spouted off just the other evening that this hiring of help is more trouble than it is worth.

The sun shines hot and the sweat rolls down my back as I wrap up the milking chores and make my way to the house for breakfast. The humidity must be 80 percent. A pickup truck is already parked in front of the house, and the sound of trowels clunking on mortar boards can be heard. Saul Schowalter and Alvin Schmutz, the two ministers from Moorland Mennonite, are busy stacking cement block upon cement block. The end result will be a new basement wall. Several other men from the church came a few days ago to help with basement cleanup. I don't think we are deserving of this help, but having the basement shored up against further rain and mud so quickly is certainly a blessing. And it seems that Pappy and Mama have reached a shaky stalemate with the church at least for now. The result is that we are again occasionally attending Sunday morning services at Moorland. Maybe it's because the pipeline project has been defeated, and Pappy has no need to participate in the protest group any longer.

In August, the Midwestern Mennonite Fellowship holds its annual tent meetings in Goshen, Indiana. It is a time of fellowship, networking, and worshipping together for Mennonites from all over the country. Attending it has always been a goal for our family, though it has only occasionally been possible. Attending provides a special highlight to the year. With the bulk of summer's work completed, Pappy and Mama decide that this year, they are going to make the trip.

"Good-bye," I wave out the dining room window as Pappy and Mama climb into the car and drive away. There are no hugs and kisses or teary good-byes. Nothing from a farm-work standpoint really changes anymore, either, when they are gone. Paul, with Joseph's help, is working on digging the foundation and then cementing it in preparation for building our sixth grain bin. For me, there is Mama's work to do—dishes to wash, meals to heat, and beds to make—but other than that, life pretty much goes on unchanged without them. What does change is that the emotional tension that always hangs in the air goes with them.

As September unfurls, Pappy's sister comes to stay for two weeks, followed by Grammy and Aunt Harriet, Mama's aunt from Pennsylvania. I love having my grandmother around. She is quiet but always treats us kindly, though I don't feel that I know her very well. During their visit, Grammy and Aunt Harriet take over the job of cooking our supper so that Mama can sleep longer in the afternoon. Mama is still working nights as a nurse in pediatrics at the hospital. It seems that Mama lives in a separate world from the rest of us. She sleeps during the day, works at night, and fits all the other tasks of cooking, cleaning, and washing into the evenings. She does not help or even seem to be aware of the farm work and conflicts that go on outside.

One evening, we all gather around the table for supper. In the center of the table, Grammy has placed a steaming pot of vegetable beef stew.

"Bless this food to the nourishment of our bodies," Pappy prays.

As I look up from the blessing, a brown creature swoops through the dining room, passing just over the table.

"Ahhhhhh! Cover the soup!" Grammy screams as she jumps up from the table.

The rest of us all begin to laugh. Having bats visit us is a common occurrence in our house, just usually not in the middle of supper. I get up and find a magazine to swat the offensive creature when he comes by again. Somehow, I have managed to become the official bat-killer at our house. While my brothers stuff towels under their bedroom doors and cover their heads when one of the winged creatures dive-bombs us in the middle of the night, I am left to get up and capture the unwelcome visitor. That is, if I want to get any sleep.

I make my stance. One well-aimed swat with the magazine, and a still-squirming creature is deposited outside. We are able to continue with our meal in peace. I just hope that Grammy hasn't been so terrorized that she won't ever want to visit again. At least, she saved the soup.

Having visitors around continuously for more than a month has certainly attenuated the tension that is often present at our supper table, but it has done little to change the atmosphere outside of the house.

The summer heat has given way to the coolness of fall. Last night, the temperature dropped to twenty-four degrees, resulting in our first hard frost. White crystals cover the ground, and the air is still frosty as Pappy heads for the cornfield south of the buildings to begin chopping corn silage on this second day of October.

I fill a bucket with soapy water and scrub each milk receiver jar in the parlor until the ringlets left by the hard water sprayed on them each day disintegrate, and a sparkle appears beneath. As I work, the sounds of everyday farming come and go outside. The 4430 John Deere sits idling by the silo. Every thirty minutes or so, the engine revs, and it is pressed into service, heaving the chopped corn into the silo. Paul comes and goes too, pulling the loaded silage wagon with the smaller 3010 John Deere tractor. Paul likes the smaller tractor, as it is easier to maneuver. He has taken it to use today, leaving the bigger 4010 John Deere tractor for Joseph. Muffled sounds rise and fall on the other side of the barn as Joseph mixes and grinds the weekly rations for the cows. He is just beginning to empty his load into the bin by the slatted free-stall barn when Pappy comes roaring into the farmyard on the chopper and jumps out. I wonder if he has broken down and decide to go investigate as to why he is coming in. I can tell by his resolute stride and stiff stance as he marches toward Joseph that he is furious. Without any preliminary, he reaches out and shoves Joseph up against the silo.

"I told you not to use this tractor for grinding feed," he shouts. "Paul needs it to pull the wagons. You always think you know better than everyone else. If you don't like the way we do things around here, go get a job at Howell's. (Howell is a local hog farmer who has a reputation for not treating his help very kindly. His operation is filthy as well.) See how long you last there."

Joseph stares at him and then turns and walks away.

"Don't walk away from me when I'm talking to you."

By now, I am furious, and my repulsion at this behavior makes me want to slap him around so he gets a taste of his own medicine. But I am powerless to stop this craziness. I am trapped in the same washing machine; just in a different rinse cycle. I do not understand my father. On the one hand, he tells Joseph on a regular basis to leave if he doesn't like the way it is. But on the other hand, he does everything in his power to keep him from having the physical or psychological skills needed to make it on his own. Always the obedient wife, Mama (if she even knows anything about it) does nothing to stop Pappy from treating Joseph this way.

The next day, Pappy has gone to town. Joseph, in a rare moment of self-assertiveness, climbs into the car and drives down the road six miles, to the Howell farm. He meekly approaches the owner and timidly asks for his first job, at twenty-two years of age. Mr. Howell, sensing his uncertainty and lack of confidence, laughs at the request. Joseph returns home downcast.

I eagerly rip open the envelope marked with the return address of Friendship High School. Inside is my high school transcript for the two years that I attended there. I need this if I want to apply to a college program. I am slowly taking concrete steps toward my dream. It is just three days after my twenty-fourth birthday. Two days ago, I finally got up the nerve to tell Pappy that I want to leave. He did not respond but turned and walked away.

Over the course of the summer, Pappy and Mama have come into contact with a young couple from Iowa who desire to become Mennonites. Pappy sees his opportunity to try again to start a Mennonite church closer to us. He and Mama personally take them under their wing. During the months of November and December, Wayne and Sheila Adler are invited to our house for Sunday school and church every Sunday. They often stay for Sunday dinner. I am not enthralled with this new arrangement. We have been involved in two church-plant attempts already since we have lived here, and neither of them has gone well. *Why should I think that this will be any different?* I really have no desire, either, to be involved in any church run by my father. I can't see any future as far as church life goes. Pappy, however, has been aware of a closed church, in a town about twenty miles east of here, that is for sale. He makes a decision to purchase this building using his own money. And on

December 29, Pappy and Mama drive to Iowa and help Wayne and Sheila move to a small farm that lies about five miles from us. Now they are close enough that we can help them daily.

December! Only one more month till I go away to Bible school. Mama has taken a three-month leave of absence from the hospital so that she will be available to help during the six weeks that I am gone. I spend my days making sure the herd health records are up to date and as many cows as possible have legible ear tags. The other job I hope to get done is moving the calves from the hutches into the new heifer barn that has just been completed.

It is sunny today, but the thermometer dipped to zero overnight. I hate cold weather. I bundle up in two coats and pull on long pants under my dress before making my way out to the barn. Our plan is to move some of the bigger hutch calves to their new home today. I push the big, two-foot-wide broom from one side of the pens to the other, over and over, until the full length of the fifty-foot barn is free of nails and leftover building materials. Paul hauls the garbage away with the skid steer and brings back a load of straw for bedding. I shake out two bales of straw for each pen. It is noon by the time the pens look inviting for their new occupants.

After dinner, Paul pulls alongside the hutches with the cattle trailer. We have decided that this method will be easier than trying to run the animals to the barn and having them run us all over the farm. Each hutch wire is pulled up and the calf captured and then wrestled up and into the trailer. There are over forty hutches with calves right now. If we can empty at least half of them, it will be easier and less time-consuming to feed the remaining hutch calves during the winter months. It is a huge task to carry water and feed to each one separately twice a day. This will also open lots of hutches for the new calves that arrive daily. We are running out of room for the calves.

Our idea of loading the calves on the trailer for transport works well until Paul tries to make a swing out into the field by the barn for unloading. He becomes bogged down in the still-unfrozen ground. By the time we get unstuck and are ready to unload, Paul is impatient and ready to be done with this. The cattle prod comes out, and there is mass chaos in the trailer before the animals decide that it is in their best interest to leap off and kick up their heels in the fresh, clean straw.

Joseph now has almost twenty hutches that need cleaning out before they freeze up. It would be so easy if he could just tip them back and scoop the manure with the skid steer. But Joseph is not allowed to drive the skid steer. He must fork out each hutch by hand with a pitchfork. This will be his job for the next couple of days.

As the end of December approaches, I begin to pack things for Bible school. I am both excited and apprehensive.

Chapter 8

BIBLE SCHOOL LEADS TO FIRST ATTEMPT AT LEAVING

J awaken to the wind whistling around the corner of the house. It is January 2, 1982, and I am leaving today for Ash Hill, Ohio. My breathing is shallow, and my stomach is doing its familiar flip-flopping as I milk. I am so afraid that something will go wrong so that I won't be able to go. It has started to snow by the time Pappy, Mama, and I climb into the car after breakfast. They will be driving me to Tomah, Wisconsin, where I am to meet up with a group of eight young folks from Dells Rapids, Wisconsin. By the time we reach the meeting place at the intersection of Interstate 90 and 94, the snow is coming down like feathers being shaken from a giant pillow. I throw my suitcase into the van, and we are soon on the way again. I am glad I am not the one driving. The continual cascade of snowflakes is making it difficult to see.

As I look around the van, I recognize most of the young people from my visit a few years earlier to Dell Rapids with our Wiehler friends. But I do not know any of them well, so I mostly sit quietly and listen to the happy chatter around me. Before I know it, my eyes close, and sleep erases the passing of time. The snow gradually turns to rain by the time we reach Illinois. Ice, mixed with the pouring rain, then pecks on the windshield. We finally stop for the night at the home of a young couple who formerly had made their home in Dell Rapids. The evening is spent singing together to the accompaniment of a guitar, laughing, and sharing stories from "home."

The next day dawns cloudy, but the rain has stopped. We stretch sleepily and yawn at eight o'clock in the morning. We have lots of time to get to our destination today (or so we think). However, when the driver turns the key of the van, the only sound that comes out is a continual cranking. The three guys and our host work on the van all morning. We are finally able to get on the road by two. The stark and dreary old two-story school building nestled away in the hills of Ash Hill, Ohio greets us when we finally arrive, around eight thirty that evening. I am tired and feeling very disconnected in this strange world. I am ready to retreat to a private corner for a while, but there is no such place here.

I follow the same pattern as the last time I went to Bible school, in Minnesota, and I roll out of bed at five thirty in the morning. This gives me time to shower and dress alone, avoiding the crush of humanity all trying to use the showers at once. We file into the chapel after breakfast, and I look around at all the other young people. Other than the Wisconsin group, I do not recognize any of them. I feel vastly alone in this sea of faces. I am one of the older students here, as most Mennonite young people are married by the age that I am, twenty-four. In fact, I am the only female student over the age of twenty-two. I do, however, recognize two of the teachers for this term, Luke Hartzler and Stanley Neufield. Brother Luke is just a little older than I am and grew up in the same congregation where we belonged in south-central Pennsylvania. He is now a minister there. Brother Stanley was another of the ministers at the same church throughout my early years there. I am comforted by this little touch of the home that I remember.

After chapel, we file out to our classes. There are four class periods, with lunch between them. This first two-week term, my class list includes Victorious Christian Living, Separation and Nonconformity, a study on the New Testament book of Mark, and a study hall. I mostly keep to myself throughout the day, but by evening, my reserve has begun to lessen. The thought that *nobody knows me; nobody knows my family here* is freeing. During free time in the evening, I climb onto the trampoline and begin to bounce. I loved to bounce in high school. Soon my heart and my face are both laughing.

The first week has gone by slowly as I struggled to make connections with the other students and get comfortable with the new environment. I find myself alone a lot and without purpose. Apparently, the only thing I really know how to do is work.

Throughout this day, students were scheduled for their term interviews with instructors. I really did not know what to say in mine. I am basically tired of sharing about home life. I want to leave my home life in another world. And I find myself coming to the end of the day feeling very discouraged.

Later in the evening, I notice that Ricky is hanging off by himself. In an effort to be friendly, I strike up a conversation with him. I learn that Ricky is also twenty-four years old and the oldest male student. Ricky further reveals that he does not come from a Mennonite background. He has recently become a Christian and is interested in joining the Mennonite church. Rumor has it that drugs and alcohol abuse were a part of his past. He seems to be mostly ignored here and I have noticed that some of the students make fun of him behind his back. There is a part of me that identifies with Ricky and makes me want to reach out to him. I know what it is like to not share the common experiences of other Mennonite young people and to feel like a total misfit in this Mennonite cultured environment.

Another week has passed and today is the last day of the first term. I feel free. There is no studying to do. I am looking forward to a quiet weekend at the school.

"Do you want to go along to Pennsylvania this weekend?" asks Luke Hartzler, the one minister from the church of my youth. I had known that a group was going east but had decided I was going to stay at the school and just hang out alone. Besides, I didn't want to intrude by asking. My heart skips a beat and I make a last minute decision.

"Just give me a few minutes and I'll throw some clothes together." I respond. Excitement is surging through me as I climb into the car. I feel pulled towards and connected to these people from my childhood. Our little group consists of Luke as our driver, two of the Wisconsin young folks, another Pennsylvania gal, Sue Ellen, and me. Sue Ellen and I, I discover, have a lot in common. We both grew up on a dairy farm in Pennsylvania. In an odd twist of providence, two of her sisters also currently live in Minnesota and are part of the Mennonite group there with whom my parents seem to be so at odds. Our common backgrounds provide many experiences for sharing during our six hour trip and the friendship that I was longing for at Bible school begins to bud.

I wake up on Saturday morning to sunshine pouring through the window of the bedroom at the home of Roy Hartzler, Luke's parents. Brother Roy is still the deacon at my childhood church. I remember him as a man of few words. And in my mind's eye, I always see an old man, dressed in his black, plain suit, sitting silently, stiffly, and ramrod-upright on the front bench during worship services.

Later that morning, I am greeted at the door of the Neufield home. Barbara, Stanley Neufield's wife, grabs my hand and lays a quick kiss on my lips, in what is known as the "holy kiss" among Mennonites.

"Wow, it's so good to see you again!"

"Would you like to see the farm?" asks Brother Stanley after lunch.

"Yes, I would like that, but I don't want you to go out of your way for me." I reply.

"Come on then."

We all climb in the car and make the twenty-mile drive out to what used to be our farm. It has been eight years. All the buildings are gone except for the house, the big old bank barn, and the free-stall barn with its two silos. A new grain setup sits in the field just opposite the old barn. Sadness steals over me as I survey the changes, and I wish again that we had never left this home, where our family once lived and worked in harmony together. Wanda, the Neufields' daughter, and I talk well into the night, reminiscing about the "old days" before sleep wraps its cloak around us.

Sunday morning, I slip into my cape dress and put my hair up into its braided, tight bun. I cover my hair with the white mesh "covering" that I wear every day. The simple brick Mennonite meeting house looks just like I remember it. We enter through the doors in the middle on the street side of the building, directly into the cloak room. The women's section of the cloak room is on the right, and the men's is on the left. From there, we silently file into our seats on the long wooden benches. The women and children will sit on the right side of the church. The men will sit on the left. Everyone sits quietly until the clock strikes 9:30 a.m. That is the signal for the song leader to get up and announce a hymn number. While everyone reaches for a hymn book and flips to the right page, the song leader brings his little round pitch pipe to his lips. He gives it a blow and begins to hum the tune. With a burst of harmonized notes and a flowing arm motion from the leader to set the timing, the congregation begins to sing a cappella along with him. After the song, everyone is dismissed to Sunday school. There are only two anterooms and one upstairs room that are used for the youngest children. The rest of the classes are separated by curtains in the main sanctuary. Soon, the air buzzes with a multitude of voices, all blending together in one big hum. A "ding" from the silver hand-held bell announces that the classes have five minutes to wrap up. Following Sunday school, more hymns are sung and then the ministers file up onto the platform together and the preaching begins. Wistfulness settles over me. Memories of old times come flooding back. Not much has changed here in eight years. I am glad that I came along on this weekend trip. After dinner at Roy Hartzler's, we head back to Emmanuel Bible School.

The first week of the second term is almost over already. I make my way from the chapel to my first class of the day, the Christian Home. *What is a Christian home?* The concept seems foreign and out of reach for me. In its place is a sense of despair that is always just a step away from overtaking me.

My other classes this term are on the Life of Elijah and Elisa and II Corinthians. Because it is Friday, classes are done by two, and a mass of laughing, chattering young people rush back to their respective dorms to prepare for whatever weekend activities that they have planned. Some, like me, are going to just hang out here over the weekend. There will be time for talking and checkers and puzzles and Ping Pong and shuffleboard. And tomorrow, I will be helping all afternoon to make cream pies for next week's desserts. Dessert is something we cannot live without.

With the passing of the weekend, classes and weekly activities resume. I am feeling much more lighthearted this afternoon, as I had an interview today, this time with the principal of the school, Jesse Gingerich. I finally made a decision to try to share some of my struggles with him and his wife. My whole story came pouring out.

"Amanda, you are twenty-four years old. You are of an age to make your own decisions. God does not require that you follow your father's wish to stay on the farm," Brother Jesse impresses on me again. "Honoring one's parents after becoming of age does not include having no choice in your life's direction."

This is hard for me to grasp, as all my life it has been stressed by the church to the young people—and definitely by Pappy— that parents know best, and if we are honoring them, we will listen to their words of advice and do as they counsel. And in my mind, a war rages. *I don't think they really understand the control that I am up against.* Jesse and his wife, Anna, offer their support and encouragement if I should wish to make a decision while I am here at Bible school.

My heart is light throughout the rest of the day. After supper, I make my way to the recreation room to hang out. A bunch of young people are already there. I smile at Ricky across the room, and he approaches me. We chat for a few minutes about the day; then he pauses.

"I have something I would like to ask you."

I search his face. He is fidgety and shifts from one foot to the other.

"Will you go on a date with me? I think you're the kind of person I am looking for in a wife."

I drop my eyes. My heart sinks, and I am speechless. *How could I not see this coming? I was just trying to be friendly, and he has interpreted my actions as something more.*

"I'm sorry. I can't right now." I spit out. I turn and walk away, leaving him standing there. My thoughts are racing. *I really do not want to hurt his feelings, but I don't have any physical attraction to the guy. And the last thing I need right now is to be involved with another messed-up person. The guys with normal backgrounds seem to shy away from me, so I am left with the misfits like me to choose from.*

I pile into the station wagon at five o'clock in the afternoon along with three other girls. Thomas Franz, an instructor, will be our driver. Our car load is completed by his wife and two small children. It is the end of my fifth week here, meaning it is the middle of the third term. Those who are here this term are divided into gospel teams. Each team goes out to different area Mennonite churches to give a program of song and testimonies during the weekend. Following us in a separate car are the five boys who are a part of this team. Our first stop tonight is at a small town in southeastern Ohio, on the Ohio River. After the service, the boys and girls again divide up for the night. We girls will be staying at the home of Karen Miller. Karen and I have grown close at Bible school, so I am looking forward to seeing where she lives. I am shocked when we stop in front of a house. It looks more like a shack. The paint is peeling. The roof is of rusting tin, and it sags. We are greeted by two blatting goats. But inside, the atmosphere is cheery though noisy. There are way too many people for such a small space, but we are welcomed with food and big hugs. We laugh and talk till one o'clock in the morning.

I am awake before the alarm goes off, and I lay there thinking. I am excited and apprehensive all at the same time. The next leg of our journey will take us to Kentucky. This is where the home of Jesse and Anna Gingerich is located. Brother Jesse has specifically gotten me onto this gospel team. He has suggested that this is an opportunity for me to visit a Mennonite Publishing House close to their home. He works with this publishing company and would be able to get me a job there if desired. I have only one more week left at Bible school in which to make up my mind. *Oh! I don't want to go back home.*

Our entire group meets at the church by ten o'clock, and we head for Kentucky. As we drive deeper into the state, I am struck by how dismal the landscape and the houses are. The hillsides are steep, and the homesteads dreary and unkempt. But then, it probably looks worse because it is February. There are neither leaves on the trees nor any snow on the ground. Five hours later, we roll into a little town hidden in the hills of southeastern Kentucky. It doesn't look like much of a town. The simple, white Mennonite church faces the main road. Close by is the home of Jesse and Anna Gingerich. Our voices echo off the surrounding hills as we volley the ball back and forth over the volleyball net in their backyard.

After our supper at the home of Larry Wiebe, a local congregational member, we return to the church to give our program. During the service, I stand and give my testimony, something that, just a few short weeks before, I would have been too ashamed to even consider.

"I thank God for allowing me to come to Bible school in Ohio for two terms. I have come to know Jesus like I never have before. My desire is to give my life to God in service once I leave Bible school. I want my life to honor Him in all I do."

I feel at home here and accepted by these people, and I have become somebody that I would never dare to be at home around my parents.

Monday includes a tour of the Mennonite Publishing House before we return to the school. I wonder what life would be like here.

"Come for a week, and see how you like it," is the offer extended to me.

Part of me wants to try this, but the other part of me knows it will not be that easy. I really don't think there is any hope of my being allowed to make such a decision.

We have been back at Bible school for a couple of days. I have fallen comfortably into the routine now, studying Personal Relationships, Mennonite History, and the book of James this term. And I have found the courage to share my struggle with all the girls. Last evening, when I pulled back the covers, I found candy hidden in my bed. I was touched. Sue Ellen admitted to the deed when I questioned her. This led to a long talk between us before bedtime. I also had another long talk with Jesse Gingerich today.

"I just don't know what to do," I anguish at lunch. Several girls gather around and pray for me. I think I have come to a decision. I am going to go to the publishing house in Kentucky instead of going home after this week. *I can imagine how this is going to be received by my determined father.* And now I have to break the news. I decide to call the folks the next day and leave them a message when no one is around.

It does not take long to get a response. Jesse Gingerich gets a phone call from Pappy the next day.

"I expect that Amanda will be home at the planned time. We have work to do here, and we can't do it without her. You have no business being involved in our affairs. I will decide what my daughter will do, not you."

My heart sinks when Jesse tells me about the phone call, but it is pretty much what I expected. Now Jesse understands too. We talk some more, and Jesse counsels, "Go home and try to talk to him, in love, about your concerns and needs. Pray that God will work in his heart and soften it."

Dream on. I have no faith that anything I say will have any impact. But I really have no choice at this point. I can't stand against Pappy alone, and in the face of his opposition, I sense the reluctance of Jesse and his wife to blatantly go against my father.

I hitch a ride from Bible school with two boys who are headed toward my aunt's home in Ohio. They drop me off at Aunt Rhonda's house late on Friday evening. The plan is to spend the weekend visiting with Aunt Rhonda and two uncles who live in the area. But the fun is over. By Sunday night, my stomach has begun to churn, and the stabbing pain has begun its creep. I lay awake in my bed, unable to sleep. I tuck a pillow under my stomach to try to stem the rising nausea, and I begin to shake. Tomorrow morning, I fly home to my miserable life. I finally get up at five o'clock and dress.

"I can't eat any breakfast," I tell Aunt Rhonda.

"But you have to eat so you have strength."

I shake my head no. "Let's just get going."

By eleven o'clock in the morning, I am landing at the international airport close to home.

Pappy does not mention anything that first day about my plan to not come home. The familiar routine begins again the next morning at four o'clock. My stomach is upset, and I feel utterly hopeless. When Pappy comes to help finish up the milking, I tell him again that I want to leave the farm. He spends an hour telling me how stupid I am to consider such a thing. He goes on and on and on. Blah! Blah! Blah! Blah! The only part I hear is, "I have

done all this for you, and now you want to leave me sit with it. If
you leave the farm, you get nothing out of the farm."

I am more angered and disgusted by his threat than anything,
as I recognize the manipulation that it is. I drag myself around all
day. I have no motivation to do anything. I go to my room to cry
and finally fall into a fitful sleep.

Chapter 9

FOUR MORE YEARS
OF STRUGGLE

A month has passed since my return from Bible school, and life has returned to its former everyday drama—with a new element added in. We have been traveling the five miles back and forth on a regular basis to the home of Wayne and Sheila Adler. The purpose of our visits is to help them get established at their new place. Wayne has decided that he wants to milk some cows in the small barn on the rented property. Pappy, who is eager to keep the Adlers in the area, finds a small herd of twenty cows that he buys for Wayne.

The clouds hang dark and heavy. The wind pushes against the already rocking cattle trailer. As I walk past the trailer and into the previously abandoned barn, drops of rain touch my face. The project of the afternoon is to help Wayne unload his newly arrived cows. As the cows are prodded off the trailer by Pappy and Paul, Wayne and I shoo them and wave our arms to encourage each one into a stanchion. Then the trick is to sneak up and slam the stanchion headlock shut before the riled-up animal decides to back out and go careening off. It takes a couple of hours to get all of the cows unloaded and secured in their new home. Once the cows are settled in, I return to do the evening milking at home. I am back at Wayne's by eight o'clock in the evening to help them wrap up their first night of dairying.

A week later, I step inside the little white church at Grand Valley that Pappy purchased in December. It is Sunday. We and Adlers are meeting for the first time at the church since the local Bible school ended last Sunday. "The Lord is coming" declares the sign on the wall behind the pulpit. Pappy stands up front to teach the Sunday school lesson, and a discussion follows. Mostly, it is a discussion between Wayne and Sheila and the folks as Pappy tries to expound to them the truth from the Bible as he sees it. *I personally see no future in this venture. All I see is hypocrisy and self-righteousness.* Just two Sundays ago, the minister at Moorland Mennonite preached on "Where does Jesus come in our value system?" *Jesus in our value system? Is Jesus in our value system?*

A rhythmic click, click, click sounds, as the head of the irrigator spouts dark-brown liquid high into the air while rotating in a circle. It is not a machine that I wish to get very close to—unless, of course, I desire a "refreshing" shower. To feed the advancing monster, a row of irrigation pipe stretches from the free-stall barn to the field south of the buildings. The setup culminates in a flexible hose that attaches to the moving irrigator. As the machine crawls across the field, the liquid manure is flung out over the land, propelled through the pipe by the pump back at the barn. The smaller John Deere tractor sends up a column of black smoke as it works to supply power to the pump. It is the first week in June, and with the corn almost planted, it is time again to empty the manure pit before the crops fully occupy the land. And this year, Pappy has decided to bring home another piece of equipment that is supposed to be faster and more efficient in performing this chore. *It is an interesting concept, but my question is, do we really need this?*

The next day, after milking, I climb into the big four-wheel-drive tractor to work the manure-covered ground so that the last of the corn can be planted. Pappy has gone to the river, hauling last year's corn. Paul is spraying for weeds in the already planted fields. The air around me reeks with that "country-fresh smell" as I turn the tractor and digger onto the field for my first pass. Brown semi-dried gruel wraps itself around all four tires, and clumps of it plop onto the windows and the hood of the tractor as the wheels go around and around. In some areas of the field, I find myself spinning, unable to move forward. I turn the steering wheel back and forth to break the tractor in the middle and wiggle myself out of the sloppy spots. It is almost too wet to work, but I keep going. *I think that machine threw way too much shit on here.* At dinnertime, Paul and I both make it very clear to Mama that neither of us likes this new method of spreading the slurry and do not want to buy the equipment. Mama assures us that she will call the bank this afternoon and stop payment on the check that Pappy has already given the dealer.

Paul is refilling the sprayer with water as I roll up to the buildings at milking time and park.

"You have crap all over my tractor," is his greeting.

I have no more than started to put the milking equipment together when I hear the grumble of the four-wheel-drive engine, and Paul pulls up outside the milk house with the tractor. Soon the swish, swish of the high-pressure washer wand going back and forth can be heard as he gives the tractor a bath. Paul is very particular about his tractors. It upsets him greatly to have mud or manure on them. By the time Pappy returns from the river to begin planting the field into corn, the manure is nicely worked into the ground, and the tractor is sparkling clean. To him everything is just fine.

The next day dawns cloudy and rainy. We have just gotten done with breakfast when the phone rings.

"Can you come and help chase the cows? They have gotten out." Wayne implores.

For the next two hours, we slip and dash through the mud and rain, corralling the escaped animals and hauling them back home to Wayne's. I really don't need someone else's extra work and find this disturbance to be trying and annoying. I have just enough time left in the morning to figure out what cows I need to dry off in the next week and then it is time for dinner. Pappy's jaw is set at the dinner table. We eat in silence for a while. Then, he clears his throat.

"I am buying the manure equipment," he announces. "I make the decisions around here, and I don't see any reason to cancel my agreement. Having your mother stop payment on the check is not going to stop me from doing what I think is best for the farm."

I am not sure why we thought we could change the outcome of something. For the next three days, Pappy won't talk to us. Meals are eaten in silence. He goes about his work with a set jaw and averted eyes, acting like we don't exist.

Several weeks later, I push back from the breakfast table. Everyone else has left the house, and Mama has not yet lain down for her nap. I take a deep breath as I approach her in the kitchen.

"Mama, can you talk to Daddy for me? I want to apply to go to school this fall. I want to do something else with my life other than milk cows."

It is early August, and I am hopeful that I can solicit the support of my mother in my venture. I hold my breath as I wait for her response. She has always sided with Pappy when I have tried to talk to her in the past about concerns and problems.

"You really just need to settle down and do as your father says. He knows what's best for you. Besides, we all have to work together if we are going to make a go of the farm."

I can feel my anger rising, and my voice rises too. "But I don't understand. You went to nursing school and became a nurse. Then you went to France for two years to work in a children's home. It was okay for you, but I'm supposed to stay here my whole life and work on the farm. Why can't I go out and experience life like you did? Your father didn't expect you to stay at home and work."

She bends her head over the dishwashing pan. "You wouldn't be able to make it on your own if you left the farm," is her response.

I can't quite believe my ears. I am totally confused. I don't understand my mother any more than I understand my father.

Turning away, I walk out the door and head to the barn. I am not much in the mood to work, but the chores are always waiting. While I work, my mind is mulling over my conversation with Mama. *Why did I think that she would be willing to stand up for me?* My jaw is clenched and my stomach still churns, but a part of me understands that she also is unable to stand up to the power and control of my father. But the other part of me expects her, as the other adult in the family, to fight for her children. And I am puzzled by her seeming inability to acknowledge that there even is a problem. After some time of contemplation, I come to another decision. *Since I can't talk to them and get anywhere, I will write a letter and put all my feelings on paper, where I can be logical and emotionally controlled. Maybe then, I can make them understand.*

As I pedal back to the house on my bicycle, I can smell the scent of freshly mown hay. Pappy is turning the hay over with the rake one more time before baling it. The baler sits parked by the garage, ready to go. The hay should be dry by milking time. That means there will be absolutely no help for milking tonight. But at least, since Pappy bought the automatic bale wagon, I don't usually need to help unload hay anymore. Pappy bales the hay on the ground. Paul follows behind, sweeping up the bales with the magical wagon. The hay unloads from the wagon automatically too, with just a touch of guidance from Paul. The bales come off, one right after the other, in sets of three, and are loaded onto the elevator. The hard job is stacking them in the mow, as there is no time for rest. Patience and empathy for the person in the mow are not virtues of Paul's either, so the mow stacker is pushed to the max in order to hustle the bales away as fast as they come up. This killer job is left to Joseph and whatever young boys they can manage to hire from the community.

I shut off the milker pump after the departure of the last cow from the parlor and push open the outer milk-house door. Curiosity draws me to see what is going on outside. Usually, someone has come to feed the cows and wash out the parlor by now. A half-unloaded bale wagon sits straddling the elevator. The tractors are silent, but I can hear the skid steer idling. I wander over to the old red barn. The problem is evident now. The heavy load from all the hay in the mow above has splintered a supporting post below. Paul and Pappy struggle to support the barn while they replace the post. *Well, I guess I might as well go back and wash out the parlor and clean up by myself.* By the time I am done, the sun has sunk below the horizon. The cows are bawling loudly for their supper. Their supper and ours don't come for yet another hour, and my bed feels really good when I finally collapse into it at midnight.

Raindrops pound on the roof. I stand just inside the mudroom door and look out into the dark, driving rain. Oh well. Here goes. I duck my head, jump on my bicycle parked just outside the door, and pedal as fast as I can to the barn. It is a Sunday morning in late August. I am drenched by the time I reach the barn. The start of school is just a month away. I still have not made any progress in getting enrolled. Just this week, Pappy and I got into another big argument over the number of cows that we have. The response I got was another sermon about how this is God's plan for my life, since God put me in this family with him as the head of it. If this is God's plan for my life, I want no part of it. But I don't believe that my father's viewpoint is from God, and even though God seems far away on this farm, I keep trusting that He will somehow work things out so that my father will see wherein he is wrong and change.

Things have not been going well in the relationship with Wayne and Sheila, either. Pappy and Mama are happy to share their knowledge of farming and child-rearing with the couple. The problem is that they then expect them to do things as they suggest. Wayne and Sheila, like any young couple, bristle at being told what to do. The tension has been rising all summer.

We finish up the milking with time to spare for a short nap before church. By the appointed time for the morning service, we are driving up to the little white church in Grand Valley. We take our place in the pews and wait for Wayne and Sheila before beginning. The clock slowly ticks in the silence. By the time its big hand has made half a journey around the face, it is evident that they are not coming. Pappy finally tells us to get in the car. Instead of having a church service, we go for a long Sunday afternoon drive through western Minnesota to see a friend.

The next day, Mama goes to visit Sheila to see if she can determine what the problem is. She wants to know why they did not show up for church and didn't even bother to call.

"We've found a dairy farm in Wisconsin and are moving there next month," Sheila tells her. "We just can't deal with being treated like children anymore."

"I'm sure you just misunderstood things. We're just trying to help you get started," Mama responds. "We really need you to stay."

But the young family is not interested in staying. They have already made their decision.

I pick up the letter from my nightstand. My hand is trembling, and I hesitate. I finally turn and force myself to hurry across the hall to Pappy and Mama's bedroom. I push open the door, drop the letter on their bed, and make my hasty retreat to my own bedroom. I try to slow my breathing down. *I feel stupid and want to disappear. I must like banging my head on the wall.*

We did not go to church today. I spent all morning writing my letter to Pappy and Mama, trying to explain the frustration, the unhappiness, the depression that I feel and begging them to let me apply to college. A couple of weeks ago, I sent off a letter requesting a brochure of correspondence courses from the University of Wisconsin-Extension. And earlier this week, I sent off a letter to the local community college requesting an application packet for the nursing program. Now I need to wait for a reply from Pappy before I can move forward. I pray, "Please Lord, make them understand. Change their hearts and minds because I just can't do this much longer."

Later that evening, we gather around the supper table for our usual Sunday-night supper of cold cereal and bologna sandwiches. I do not look at Pappy but pull out my book and start to read. Pappy clears his throat, and I glance at him.

"I bought this farm for you guys. I expect that all of you will pull your weight. I can't have you going to school and then going running off. If you want to go to school in case, later in life you need an occupation if something happens here, I guess I can live with that. But I expect that your going to school will not interfere with your work here. I can't afford to hire someone to replace you."

"All right," is all I dare say. This is not a full-fledged endorsement of my going to school, but he has at least opened the door just a crack. I have every intention of wedging my foot in.

I waste no time in the next week filling out an application for the nursing program at the community college and placing it in the mail. I wait a month, but I receive no response. Anxiety and tension fill my days. *How am I going to make this work and still keep up with all the work at home?* Part of me wants to just give it up, but another part of me is driven onward. *I will spend my whole life here if I don't do something. I don't want to look back on my life when I am fifty years old and regret that I missed out on all of life.*

The day before my twenty-fifth birthday, I borrow the car and drive to the college to talk to the dean.

"Your application for the nursing program was rejected," she tells me. "Your diploma is from an unknown correspondence school. If you want to just sign up for and take some single classes, we can see how you do. Maybe you can reapply again in a year or two."

My past of dropping out of school after tenth grade has come back to haunt me. I go home feeling very downcast. It is too late to sign up for any fall classes at the college. I need to move on to plan B. I order a freshman English correspondence class from the University of Wisconsin. This, at least, I can work on at home. *Maybe it's better this way, anyway, for this fall.*

We have not met again at Pappy's church as a Mennonite group since the day that the Adlers did not show up. Instead, we have attended services a couple of times at another community Bible church in Garvin, a small town fifteen miles southeast of the farm. On most Sundays, we have not gone to church at all. I like it at the Bible church very much. Pastor Dennis Payne is friendly and outgoing. He draws me right into the lively worship. But we must look very strange, being the only Mennonites attending a church where everyone else dresses like the community.

I realize that our latest attempt at starting our own Mennonite group is truly over when Pappy rents out the Grand Valley church building to another nondenominational group that wishes to start a Bible church in that town. And thus begins a period of time where we alternate between worshipping with the new group in Grand Valley and the group in Garvin, really having no roots anywhere.

The calendar has already flipped into November. Harvest this year is slow. The rain pours down every day or so, causing the corn to tumble over into a twisted tangled mass that obscures whatever rows there used to be. The combine crawls along at a snail's pace as Pappy attempts to pick up as much of the down corn as possible. The sun does peek out today, but the combine sits idle in the shed. The burner has gone bad in the dryer, and it needs to be replaced. Paul works on that project most of the day. I climb into the 4430 John Deere to chop cornstalks. Chopping the stalks will make it easier for Paul to plow when he finally gets around to the task. As I drive up and down the endless rows, chomping up the standing stalks, I can see Joseph and Mark picking up the sections of manure pipe from the recent cleaning out of the manure pit. Pappy has at least hired a young man to help with the harvest. Pastor Payne from the Garvin church came by with Mark a couple of weeks ago and asked if Pappy could give him a job. Pappy's first response was, "No way." But he has relented, after realizing that we are barely crawling along with our progress this fall. This whole year has been lousy and nerve-wracking from a farming standpoint. The combine finally roars to life late in the afternoon.

The next day is another miserable, rainy day. The combine sits idle again. Mud oozes from everything. But the rain also means I have a day to work on my English. I received the book and the lessons the other day in the mail, and I am eager to get started. I spend the whole afternoon, and more time after milking, working on my first assignment. This is going to take a lot longer than I was hoping. Getting done seems like an unattainable task. *But I must just take it one day at a time, doing what I can, every time I can get at it.*

The cold takes my breath away as I step out of the house a couple of weeks later. I peer at the thermometer. Five degrees below zero. I groan. The four inches of snow that fell a couple of days ago still covers the ground. I am so tired of trying to pick corn. We went from mud to fighting the cold and snow. Today, I cling to the steps of the combine with one hand while clutching a pitchfork in the other. The combine crawls along a few feet into the mess of rows crisscrossing each other. I jump down and lift the stalks so that the gathering chains on the corn head can grasp them and pull them into the harvesting mechanism. I stumble along beside the green monster all morning as we inch along. I am exhausted by noontime. There is just too much snow, and the corn is down too much to be able to make decent progress. Pappy parks the combine in the shed in the hope that the weather will moderate in a day or two, at least enough to finish.

I am both excited and tense as I go about the milking on this fourth day of January in the new year of 1983. Tonight is my first class at the community college. I went two weeks ago and signed up for a chemistry class for winter quarter. The class meets on Tuesday and Thursday evenings for four hours. That should be workable. After dinner, I steal away upstairs to my room to work on English assignment number seven. I am required to read an article and then analyze the points made in it by answering several questions. It has been a long time since high school, and I struggle with the wording and paragraph structure. I write and then I rewrite and rewrite some more, until each assignment is finally ready for typing. I am making progress, but I am not even halfway through the course yet. There are twenty assignments all together, and they each require six to eight pages of typed essay.

Chemistry class starts at six o'clock this evening. I start the milking a half-hour early and leave Joseph to finish. Hopefully, Paul and Pappy will come to help clean up too. As I drive to class, I try to calm the rapidly fluttering butterflies in my stomach. At least I made it out the door without a huge ruckus tonight. I sit quietly at a lab table while the professor introduces the class and goes over the expectations. I feel so out of place here. But the class sounds interesting. I have always loved math and detail.

The first two weeks of classes have passed quickly. I can tell by the coolness of the bathroom as I dress this morning that the wind must be out of the south. That means it will be cold in the parlor too, in spite of the heat being blown in from the furnace. The thermometer sits at twelve degrees below zero. With the wind-chill factor, it feels like twenty-five below. I shiver. The wind cuts right through me as I hustle to the barn. I quickly do a walk around through the dry cows before I get started with the milking. I want to make sure that none of them are about to calve. There are several cows due in the next couple of days. With it as cold as it is, a newborn calf would freeze to death if born out in the free-stall barn. I identify four cows that look like their pelvic muscles have relaxed since last evening, but calving does not appear imminent in any of them. I should be able to milk first and then come back and get them into the calving room/sickroom.

I hurry back out after breakfast. There is no time for a nap this morning. I round up the four animals that I identified earlier as possibly calving today and run them into the room. One heifer looks like she might already be in labor. I make a last check on her before returning to the house. Sure enough, one leg is turned back. Once I have retrieved the offending leg, I get the calf puller and ratchet the calf out. It flops, lifeless, on the floor. I am too late. Two more calves are born after lunch. They need to be fed. And then there is the room to clean up. There is no time for studying today. My stomach is tied in a knot, my back hurts, and I am exhausted. I hurry as much as I can with the milking, but I still find myself leaving a half-hour late. Tonight is my chemistry lab.

This is not the night to be late, but there is nothing I can do about it. Everyone is starting their lab assignment by the time I arrive. I am flustered and embarrassed when all eyes turn my way. I do the best that I can to quietly get organized quickly.

The next day, I feel overburdened. The calving pen is a mess from the previous day. I wash out the pen and room and re-bed it for the next animal that looks like she will calve today. After getting her settled in the fresh, clean pen, I flop on my bed. I try to study, but my eyes close and my head nods. Finally, I give in to the force that overwhelms me. Groggily, I drag myself back out to check on the cow's labor progress after dinner. Another newborn calf lies lifeless.

"How are we supposed to build up our herd when you let all the heifer calves die? You should have gotten out here sooner to check on her," Pappy admonishes when he sees the lifeless body sprawled out in front of the milk house.

"All you think about is your farm and your money. You couldn't care less about us." I snap back at him. Now I have set off the bomb. Pappy's eyes spit fire and his jaw locks into its set position as he spins and walks away. I cannot stop the tears that spill down my cheeks, into the continuing river of misery that envelopes me.

The clouds hang heavy, threatening rain. April has arrived. I have just an hour after breakfast to bed the hutches and mix some supplemental minerals for the cows before I need to leave for class. Biology class starts at ten in the morning. I finished up my chemistry class with an A in mid-March and then went to sign up for biology for spring quarter.

"The class is already full." I was told.

I stood there stunned, not sure what to say. I must have looked really crestfallen because the counselor finally said, "Just a minute. We could let you attend a few sessions and see if someone might drop out. Students have two weeks to make schedule changes, and often classes are dropped."

"Okay, I will try that." I pray that someone will drop out, because there is no other class that will work for me this semester. By the beginning of the second week, I am in. Biology class is three days per week, one more than the chemistry class I took last semester. At least, it is during the day, so milking time is not encroached upon.

I climb up into the straw mow and toss out ten bales. I stack them three high on the wheelbarrow and wheel them, bumping and swaying, over the ruts to the line of waiting hutches. Divide the bale into three, toss the segments in, climb over the fence, crawl in bent over, shake it up, and then move on to the next hutch is the order of the process. There are thirty hutches to bed right now. I force myself, every week, to repeat this exercise.

The rain begins as I climb into the car for the drive to school. Rivers of water cascade down the windshield. At least I got the calves bedded before this started. My drive is punctuated by slapping windshield wipers and pounding raindrops. I try to run through some of the lesson material while I drive. Our first test in biology is today. This also means that there won't be any new material to learn, and class should be short. I usually can zip right through tests. Then I should be on my way home again.

Beep. Beep. Beep. *Oh no! Not the alarm already.* I slowly roll out of bed. I am just as tired as I was last evening. Exhaustion has become my normal state of mind and body. The air feels cold for May, and the stars are hidden behind a blanket of clouds as I force my feet to find their way to the barn. I am dreading milking because we are in the midst of another calving spurt. This means more animals to run through the parlor, more cows to treat for sickness, and more little mouths to feed. Just the other day, I counted 190 milking cows. The sun is high in the sky by the time I finally wrap up the milking and head for the house. There is no time to allow the tension bands wrapped around my stomach and chest to relax. Class starts in an hour and a half.

I arrive home from biology just in time to eat Mama's home cooked noon meal. I am tired and looking forward to my afternoon nap.

"I need you to work some ground this afternoon," Pappy says.

My heart sinks, and I sigh. The four-wheel-drive with the digger awaits me by the garage. I pull myself up into its seat high above the world and begin the endless process of driving up and down the field. Most days, I actually enjoy driving the tractor, but today, a dark cloud of weariness hangs over me that I can't shake. I really want to spend some time studying too. But Pappy gives no consideration to such things, and I dare not ask. I soon find myself in snooze mode as I nap and weave my way up and down the field.

Milking time comes all too soon. The long process of extracting the milk from each cow begins again. I glance into the sickroom as I walk down the return alley on my way to get the cows around. The pen is brown with dirty, wet straw. Numerous manure piles litter the stall area. I make a mental note to clean up and wash out the pen after the milking is done. I don't think there are any cows that will calve tonight, so I could leave it until tomorrow, but my life feels that much more disorganized and overwhelming when I am not prepared.

With the milking done, I hurry to get the room cleaned up before going to the house. I am just finishing up with loading the wet straw onto the wheelbarrow when Pappy comes by to see why I have not come to the house yet for supper. He scowls when he sees what I am doing.

"This isn't the time to be washing out the room. If you wouldn't go running off to school all the time, you would have had time this morning to clean it up. This notion in your head is ridiculous. I need you here to help get the work done. You won't make a good nurse anyway."

I wait for him to walk away and then allow the tears to begin their creep. I slump in the chair in the office and lay my head on the desk while sobs shake my whole being. *Forget the supper.*

A couple of weeks go by. It is early June. The weather has turned hot and sunny. I took my biology final just three days ago, so classes are done for the summer. I am kind of proud of myself. I got 118 out of 125 questions correct on the final. Now, I will have just my English correspondence to work on in my "free" time this summer. The corn is almost planted as well. All that is left is an eighty-acre field that Pappy and the boys have been making hay off of before plowing it up and planting it into corn.

The smell of fresh hay touches my nostrils in the still, early-morning June air. My first stop of the day is the calving room just off the parlor. It looks like mass chaos. One new calf romps in the pen with his mother, but another protrudes halfway out of an exhausted, heaving cow. Its tongue is huge and swollen. I grab the feet and pull, wiggling the body back and forth to relieve the hip lock. The calf is soon out but lies limp and lifeless at my feet. Two upside-down feet protrude from the third cow. My experience instantly identifies them as hind feet. Backward calves are never born by themselves. Therefore, before I can begin the milking, this calf needs to be pulled as well if I am to avoid another dead calf. Our late start and the additional new calves result in not getting to the house again until close to nine. I am so strung out that I sit at the breakfast table and cry. Everyone has eaten already and gone except for Mama. She lies on the couch, sleeping. I eat my shoofly pie between sobs and retreat to my room. Mama doesn't even notice or acknowledge my tears.

An hour later, I drag myself back to the barn. I will need to "clean" a cow if she has not done it herself by now. It is not uncommon for cows to retain the afterbirth after calving, and it needs to be removed manually if the cow is not to become infected and sick. I have figured out how to do this myself, which avoids the need to call the veterinarian for this common problem, but it is hard physical work. I am wringing wet and shaking after spending an hour on this project. Then I clean up the room and get another cow in to calve. This cow presents us with a set of twins during evening milking. *Oh! I could fall flat on my face.*

The hot summer has moved into the cooler days of fall. The only new building project on the farm this year was the construction of a barn for hay storage. School wise, I have managed to finish all the assignments of my English correspondence course. All I need to do to get credit for it is to schedule a day at the college for the final exam to be proctored. I have scheduled the test for October 4 at 9:45 a.m. Then I can start working on my psychology correspondence course. I won't be taking any classes at the local college this fall semester, so that

I will be available at home to help with harvest. It is just easier for everyone that way.

I trudge to the barn in the early morning hours on test day and go about my usual routine of putting the milkers and equipment together. Soon the cows are making their way into the parlor, and the milk flows into the receiver jars. After each row has been milked, I hit the air button that releases the milk to the main holding tank in the parlor pit. The pump kicks in and pushes the milk through the overhead stainless-steel pipe into the milk house. I have milked two groups of cows before I make a dash into the milk house to retrieve a bucket. I stop short inside the milk-house door. A stream of white courses across the floor from the wash tubs toward the drain in the floor. My breathing stops. My legs turn to rubber. A wave of heat spreads outward, engulfing me. *How did this happen?* In my hurry to get started this morning, I must have forgotten to move the pipe from the wash position over into the milk tank. The result is that I have just pumped the milk from one hundred twenty cows down the drain. There is no way to hide this disaster from Pappy.

"What happened in the milk house?" Pappy questions when he comes through the parlor to feed the cows. I sense the waves of displeasure that his brown eyes send my way, though I do not turn to look at him.

I direct my answer at the cow's udder. "I guess I forgot to move the pipe to the tank this morning, and some of the milk went down the drain." My answer is purposefully evasive, as I am too mortified to reveal the extent of the damage done.

"Well, if you didn't have your head in that school stuff all the time instead of on your work, you might not make so many mistakes that cost us money."

When I don't respond, he turns and walks away, the parlor door banging behind him.

I speed toward town at nine thirty. I check my watch every few minutes. I don't want to be late for my scheduled English test time. My mind is swirling with the disastrous events of the morning. *How am I ever going to concentrate to write an essay when I am in such an uproar?* I take a deep breath in an effort to calm my frenzied emotions. *Please, Lord, help me!* My stomach is snarled in a tightly pulled knot. I sense the beginning of the familiar stabbing pain, but I can't worry about that right now. I have to pass this test.

The Chevy truck loaded with corn comes roaring up the drive as I make my way to the house on this sunny, late-October morning. Andrew Wiehler is at the wheel. I wave at him as he goes by. He is on his way to dump the load into the unloading auger at the dryer before returning for the next load. Andrew came a week ago to help with the fall harvest. I am thrilled. It takes a huge load off of me. Pappy has been out combining for a couple of hours already this morning, and he is making great progress. Thankfully, this fall is totally different from last fall. The corn moisture is low, at about 18 to 20 percent. The corn literally pours through the dryer on its way to the storage bins. Less money spent on LP gas for drying means more profit for us and a speedier harvest. My job is to keep an eye on the dryer and make sure everything is operating properly.

Since watching the dryer only requires periodically checking the corn moisture and making sure that the corn does not hang up anywhere, I have scheduled the veterinarian to come this morning. I need to get some calves vaccinated for brucellosis and some cows checked for pregnancy. The vet and I spend most of the morning on these tasks. I make a quick check of the dryer after he leaves. Everything seems in order, so I go back to the barn to "clean" a cow that has retained her afterbirth. I am able to make one more check of the dryer before everyone gathers for dinner.

"How often have you checked on the dryer this morning?" Pappy asks while we eat.

"Twice," I reply.

"It needs to be checked every hour. You can't just ignore it because you have other work to do," Pappy lectures.

Whatever. No matter what I do, it's never quite good enough.

After dinner, Andrew and I chat while he unloads his next load. My spirit always lifts when I am around him, and I find myself seeking him out to talk whenever we are free. Over the course of the next month, we spend many hours talking in the evening. Sometimes, our social chats include Paul. At other times, just Andrew and I talk. I have begun to realize that I look forward to seeing him every day. I crash into a funk when he is gone for the weekend. *This is ridiculous.* I scold myself. *There is no future in this for me. It's stupid to be in love with someone who doesn't care.* But I can't stop myself. The last night that Andrew is at our house, Paul, Andrew, and I laugh and talk well into the night. Then he is gone. I ask myself why I never expressed any of my feelings to him. In my heart, I know the reason. There is no way that I can marry someone as long as I am stuck here on the farm. My whole life would be controlled to the max, and I can't live that way.

Time has crossed into another year: 1984. With the start of the local area Bible school, ministers from different communities again descend to teach for short time periods. This morning, I found out that Brother Keith Stauffer is planning to visit us this afternoon. Brother Keith was the third minister at the congregation where we grew up in Pennsylvania. I am excited and look forward to seeing him. Joseph and I have talked to him at various times over the last few years, seeking support. I know he is an advocate for us.

A few weeks ago, Joseph, at twenty-four years of age, filled out an application to attend the Bible school this winter and mailed it in. When his acceptance came in the mail, Pappy was furious.

"You are not going to Bible school. I can't have another person running off. It wouldn't do you any good, anyway. You don't listen to anything I say, so why would you listen to the teachers?"

Pappy picked up the phone that day and called Saul Schowalter, the acting principal, at the Bible school.

"You can just take Joseph off of your list. He did this without my permission, and he isn't coming to Bible school."

I suspect that Brother Keith is coming to talk to Pappy about this incident. My suspicions will prove to be well-founded. He is concerned about the effect that Pappy's approach to the farm is having on us, his children. Keith expresses these concerns and also impresses on Pappy the importance of Joseph being able to spend some time away, studying the Bible.

"What I allow my children to do is my business. I never went to Bible school, and I turned out all right," is Pappy's response.

Thirty degrees below zero, declares the thermometer on the garage on this mid-January day. The cold makes life so much more difficult all the way around. Everything is stiff and refuses to move, including the starter on the car. We do not have an engine block heater or a garage to park the car in. The starter barely clicks when I turn the key. *I can't be late for school. I have a test in English lit.* Frantically, I search for Paul to help me get the car started.

Paul is always willing to help when things are going awry. Finally, with a little booster help, the car roars to life. "The bill will be in the mail." He chuckles, as I am off to another day of classes.

Winter semester began on January 3. I signed up for two courses this semester so I have class four days per week. I have an English literature and fiction class from eleven o'clock until noon. Then I move into anatomy from one o'clock until three o'clock in the afternoon. Having two classes means that I am driving forty to fifty miles, round trip, almost every day. On top of that, I am trying to keep up with the dairy chores between milking and class and milking again. My attempts to study usually end up with me falling asleep. At least I have a new electric typewriter now to type my papers. I got it for Christmas from Mama. What a pleasant surprise. Before, I was pecking away on Mama's old 1940s manual one.

The sun shines warm on my back as I steer the 3010 John Deere alongside the liquid manure irrigation pipe. Paul and Joseph each grab an end of the next ten-foot section and heave it onto the wagon I am pulling. Then I let out the clutch and drive ahead another few feet, while they grab the next section of pipe. And so it goes, as the little caravan creeps across the field. We are picking up the pipe after another emptying of the manure pit. Since I do not have a class to go to today, I have been pulled in to speed up the process. Corn planting was in full swing and has been halted just long enough to do the spring cleaning of the pit.

Once the last section is stowed on the wagon, Paul takes over. I return to my previous day's plan. All forty hutches are full, so I need to remove the ten oldest calves and move them into the heifer barn. Pappy made room there last week by hauling three pens of the oldest heifers to a pasture that he has rented, over sixty miles away. Now I will have a place to put the three babies that are crowded into a little three-foot-by-three-foot pen in the east free-stall barn. I throw a halter on each calf in turn and partly wrestle, partly guide the three-hundred-pound animals to their new home. Getting one's feet stepped on with sharp little toes seems to be part of this process. Once I release them into the open pen, they kick up their heels, jumping and bucking in glee.

I have just an hour or so left to rest and study my physiology before it will be time to milk again. I have taken only one class this spring semester, a physiology class, but it still requires driving to town three days per week. I am slowly making my way through the University of Wisconsin psychology correspondence course as well. I am coming to the conclusion that correspondence courses are a whole lot more work than just going to class and sitting there. The only advantage for me is that I can fit them in during little increments of time that do not disrupt my seemingly all-important work schedule.

As I make my way to the barn, I see that the four-wheel-drive tractor and digger, piloted by Paul, is working the newly spread manure into the ground. Pappy is loading corn into the hopper on the planter in preparation for planting the ground behind his son. After getting the milking equipment together, I walk out into the barn, as I do every night, to get the first group of cows around into the holding area.

The first group that we always milk is the low producers. Pappy has always run a bull with this group for clean-up purposes. Most of our cows are bred by artificial insemination, but there are always some cows that are very difficult to get pregnant. They eventually end up in this group with the bull, in the hope that he can do naturally what we cannot seem to accomplish the

artificial way. I have always hated Holstein bulls because they
cannot be trusted. This bull, in particular, has shown a tendency
toward maliciousness. He will stalk along the head of the middle row of free stalls and peek through the crack, calculating
his attack on his unsuspecting target. After Joseph was pushed
through the gate last week by this bull's charge, Pappy put a ring
in the bull's nose with a chain. This causes him to hold his head
up in the air when he walks. Hopefully, this contraption will
discourage any charging.

I glance around the barn to determine the bull's whereabouts
before I swing open the center gate to allow cows into the holding
area. I do not want to meet him face to face. He is at the far end
of the barn, so I should be safe. The center gate that divides the
groups is a steel, twenty-four-foot telescoping structure. Because
of its heavy weight, it is suspended by a cable from a roof truss of
the barn. I push the gate all the way open against the end wall.
Then I turn to walk back through the group of cows that are
making their way into the holding area. Suddenly, I stop and step
back. Mr. Bull is making his way around as well. But instead of
going on by, he advances toward me. Frantically, I try to decide
what to do. I am pretty sure I can't outrun him. Behind me is the
wall. There is nowhere to go. Then it comes to me. Climb the gate.
I scramble up, grabbing the supporting cable with my hands just
in time to realize that my feet are being knocked out from under
me by his huge, swinging head.

"Help! Help! Help!" I scream over and over. I know no
one is going to hear me. *What am I going to do?* I can't dangle
from this cable forever. My screams do attract the attention
of the meandering cows, though. Curious creatures that they
are, they all gather around to see what the commotion is all
about. Sixty sets of shining eyes look up at me. And by their
response, they distract Mr. Bull. He wanders away to sniff

for a more interesting scent. I don't think I have ever been so thankful for a bunch of cows before. I begin to tremble and my knees shake. My only thought is that I need to get down from here before he decides to come back. I slam the gate shut. My legs collapse under me, and I sink onto the floor of a stall, where I attempt to control my breathing and the uncontrollable shaking.

Friday, the first day of June dawns hot and sunny. The weather has been beautiful, and the corn planting was completed in record time. The only planting that remains is that of the soybeans. Paul is already working the ground to prepare the seedbed by the time I wrap up the milking. I stop by the planter on the way to the house and pour the bagged soybeans into the hoppers for Pappy. If the weather stays nice, the soybeans should also be planted in just a couple of days. I have just enough time to return to the barn and clean a cow before I need to head out to physiology class. We have a test today, our last test of the semester, but I never worry about passing. I ace most of my tests.

A new calf awaits me on my arrival home. I make sure it is fed before I drive to the field to see if I can help Pappy with anything before I need to milk.

"What are you doing out here?" His eyebrows scrunch together, and his face is dark. "I needed you to drive tractor this morning, not now. This school business is totally getting in the way of farming. We have to work while the sun shines—not when you get ready."

I can feel my anger rising. I feel like I have been stabbed in the heart.

"It's always about you and your stupid farm, isn't it?" I shout

at him. I turn and climb back into the car and drive away. *Fine!*
I won't help then.

Fall is fast approaching and the air has turned cooler. Paul and
Pappy have been chopping hay for the silo the last few days. The
corn and soybean crops are not quite mature enough for harvest
yet. As I open my eyes in the pitch darkness of early morning,
the soft sound of raindrops on the porch roof outside my window
reaches my ears. I shake my head to clear my brain. Oh yes. Today,
September 12, I have an appointment at the college to take my
supervised psychology correspondence course final. I have already
ordered the sociology course that I plan to work on this fall. Then
maybe one more winter and spring of taking classes at the college,
and I can reapply to the nursing program. I have made As in all
of my courses so far, so I think I should be able to get in. Though
slow, I am making progress. *Maybe it's better this way anyway. I*
wouldn't have been able to handle all the courses and the nursing sched-
ule and still take care of the cows.

October 14: my twenty-seventh birthday.

"Come on up front here so we can sing 'Happy Birthday' to
you," Pastor Payne calls from the platform.

My birthday falls on Sunday this year, and we have come to
church services at Garvin. I hold back. I can feel the heat in my
ears, and I am sure that I am turning red. I am embarrassed by all
the attention, or so I tell myself. I think I am more embarrassed by
what I perceive to be the scowling disapproval of Pappy. Such displays are seen by him as pride-producing and totally unnecessary.

Oh well! I stand and walk to the front to accept the "Happy Birthday" song directed at me. After church, we are all invited to the pastor's home for dinner, followed by cake and ice-cream. My heart is light as we drive home. It feels good to be recognized by somebody as special just because. I battle every day to counteract the little voice in my head that constantly whispers *you're nobody. Nobody cares about you. Even your father only cares about how much work you can do.* Enjoy the moment, I tell myself, for tomorrow, birthdays will be forgotten. We will be back to the business of harvesting the crops as fast as we can before winter sets in.

I try to catch my breath as I walk into the wind on the way to the barn. Rain lashes against my face, causing me to turn and walk backward every couple of steps in an attempt to suck in some air. Just two days ago, we had five inches of snow. Now the snow has all been washed away by the driving rain on this mid-December day. Harvesting is done. As we enter our "slow time" of the year, I can begin to think about what to do this winter. Just this week, I went and signed up for three classes that will begin in January. I will be taking English: writing-library source, general psychology, and efficient reading.

We finish the chores on this Sunday morning, but Joseph has not come in from scraping stalls by the time we should be leaving for church. Paul, Mama, and I decide to make our way to Garvin to church. But Pappy, instead of going with us and just leaving Joseph at home, has decided to go spy on him. I am sure there will be a huge fight, which will result in Joseph just going slower. This will only make Pappy madder. Then Pappy will turn up the volume, add a few more insults, and finally add some pushing to show him who is the boss.

The service lifts me up as it always does. I notice too in the bulletin that the Christmas program at church is tonight at six o'clock. I really want to do something different this year to celebrate Christmas. I wonder, if I ask Joseph, if he will come with me. I knock on his bedroom door when we get home.

"Will you come with me to the Christmas program at Garvin tonight?"

"Oh … I don't know," he hesitates.

"Come on. Let's get away from here for a change."

"All right," he finally agrees.

"We need to start milking early so we can get done on time," I remind him.

Pappy is secluded behind his own bedroom door, sleeping. I steal as silently down the stairs as I can, more than an hour early. I do not want to deal with Pappy's unpredictable mood. I start the milking alone, while Joseph feeds all the young stock and calves. Then he comes to help me finish up. I am on cloud nine as we cruise away to the program. Together, we are free to enjoy the fun. There is no critical eye following us tonight.

Pappy is sitting in his rocking chair when we get home, reading his Bible. He looks up at us.

"I think it is time that we all stop going to church at Garvin. You children are getting too involved there. It's one thing to go to Sunday morning services there, but I won't have you being involved in other things. You're starting to be drawn in by their ways. We are Mennonites, and we hold certain principles dear that these people do not."

I stare at him, not quite believing the words coming from his mouth. If I dared, I would laugh out loud in his face.

"And," he continues, "in the future, there will be no starting chores before four o'clock in the evening. It just messes up the animals and lowers production."

I turn and climb the stairs to bed. There is no point in responding. Sometimes I can get away with milking early to go places, but not ever if Joseph is involved.

Just a week later, on the last Sunday of 1984, we drive to church at Grand Valley. Peter Wiehler, who came last night from northern Minnesota to visit us, accompanies us to church. This is probably the biggest crowd this little church has seen in the last two years. Sadly, it is also the last Sunday for the struggling Bible church before the doors close forever. We have one final fellowship meal after the service. Then the key turns in the lock for the last time. And thus ends our two year stint of attending non-Mennonite churches.

Friday, January 11, 1985. It is the end of the first week of winter semester at the college. I am beginning to realize that going to class four days per week is going to take its toll on me. I have English, psychology, and reading on Monday, Tuesday, Thursday, and Friday. My first class of the day, English, starts at ten thirty. Today, we are to meet in the library to work on researching our topics. And then there is a crime story to read and a contrast paper to write in the next couple of weeks. Psychology looks like it should be pretty easy. I make a mental note to myself to stop at the dean's office before I go home to talk about my potential for being accepted into the nursing program. I need to get some information on scholarships and financial aid too. I sent my application in last fall, but have heard nothing back as of yet.

My visit to the dean's office later leaves me with some discouraging news. Financial aid of any kind would be based on my parents' income, since I am still living at home. It doesn't seem to matter that I am twenty-seven years old, own nothing, and have basically no income. Their assets and income are way too high for me to qualify for anything. I also know that Pappy is not about to help me voluntarily. And I am not about to give him the opportunity to use the issue to prevent me from following my dream. The dean did tell me that the letters of acceptance or rejection should be coming out in a few weeks.

In preparation for what I hope will be my acceptance into the nursing program, I went a couple of weeks ago and opened my first checking account at the bank. Now I can write checks instead of going and getting cash out of my savings account every time I need to pay tuition. At least I have the one hundred dollars that I have been putting into savings every month for the last eight years. I have now accumulated close to $10,000. I am hoping that this is enough to pay for all my tuition and books for the next three years of school. If I keep living at home, it should be.

It is a sunny and fairly warm day for mid-February. The days in the winter semester have ground slowly by. Just a week ago, I finally got my letter of acceptance to the nursing program. I am not sure if I should be thrilled or horrified. This semester has been exhausting. Work, sleep, go to class, study, work some more. I no sooner arrive home today than the vet pulls up to the barn to treat a cow with a displaced abomasum. I spend the afternoon helping to roll and position the uncooperative animal for the surgery. Then it is time to milk. I am feeling like I am at the end of my rope as I trudge to the house after chores.

My eyes turn toward a brown 1965 Mercury parked in front of the garage. *I wonder who is here. It must be some old guy, as old as the car is.* But nobody extra seems to be in the house. Pappy is sitting in his chair reading.

"Whose car is that?" I ask.

He smiles. "I bought the car for you to go back and forth to school with. It only has fifty thousand miles on it."

I am not sure what to think. There has to be an ulterior motive in this somewhere, but I decide not to ask.

"Thank you so much!" I think that is the appropriate response, though I expect any minute for Pappy to attach some strings to this "gift."

Winter semester classes ended yesterday. I passed all my finals with flying colors. I am looking forward to a two-week break before the start of the spring semester. The classes I will be taking are introduction to literature and developmental psychology. There is not a lot happening with the general farm work this time of year, either, so I am looking forward to a more relaxed schedule. Maybe there will be a little more help with the milking for a few weeks, anyway. This morning, though, when Joseph goes out to get the second group of cows around while I finish up with the first group, he comes back with some mind-numbing news.

"The cows kicked a cover off of the manure pit as I was getting them around. A whole bunch jumped over the hole, and I have no idea how many fell in."

My heart sinks into my feet. *Not again! So much for my nice, peaceful day.* This time, the pit is not empty, either. There is at least four feet of liquid manure in it. Joseph goes off to the house to get Pappy and Paul. The milking comes to a screeching halt.

Pappy peers into the dark under-floor cavern through the pit opening and shines a flashlight around. He counts two sets of shining eyes moving around in the vast sea of liquid. They must be swimming, as there is no way that the animals could be touching the bottom. There is also no way to determine if any cows have already drowned. The next problem is how to get the unfortunate beasts out. It is out of the question for anyone to go down into the pit after them. The decision is made that Paul, Joseph, and I will poke long sticks through the slats in the floor in an effort to encourage the animals to swim toward the open hole. There, Pappy will be waiting with a lasso. The whole operation is risky for everyone involved. I can feel the familiar knot forming in my stomach. All my muscles are tense with the intensity of the situation. After an hour of several close passes by the hole, Pappy is able to lasso the first cow. Now, there is no time to waste if we are to get her out before she drowns herself struggling against the rope. The rope is thrown over the barn rafter and then fastened to the backhoe. Pappy drives ahead pulling the cow up by the head while Paul and Joseph guide the rope so that she comes up through the opening and doesn't get caught.

"Go! Go!" Paul screams as the bug-eyed, struggling cow appears. She soon lies sprawled on the floor.

It takes another hour to capture the other evasive creature. Her swimming has gotten slower and more sluggish.

"If we don't get her out of there soon, she is going to drown." Paul states what we are all thinking. I am starting to feel sick to my stomach and woozy. Finally, the lasso finds its target, and she is ready for lifting out too. The tractor moves ahead. A loud crack splits the air, followed by a piece of rafter cascading from the sky. The cow disappears with a splash, back into the foul liquid.

"We have to get her out of there now!" shouts Pappy.

This time, the rope is hooked directly to the backhoe bucket and the lift begins again. The backhoe is much slower, and we all hold our breath until the filth-covered animal lies sprawled on the floor, panting. Neither cow shows any long-term effects from her ordeal. I can't say that that is true of me. I am shaking, and I have no energy to go on with the day.

A trauma of much greater magnitude occurs just a month later. It is a Sunday morning in mid-April. With all the calves being born, Mama, at sixty-one years of age, has started coming to the barn to help with feeding calves when she is not working at the hospital. Mama is not a farmer. She has always taken care of the housework and brought in income by nursing but never involved herself in the day-to-day operation of the farm.

This particular morning, I glance at the cow in the calving pen before we begin the morning chores. She is stomping around the pen, but birthing does not appear imminent. Joseph and I begin the milking, periodically checking to see how the cow is progressing. Finally the calf is born around five o'clock. I send Joseph to feed the newborn with a bottle of colostrum that I have been heating in the milk house. Mama, her short plump figure topped by a sunbonnet, appears in the milk-house doorway.

"Where's Joseph?" she asks.

I point toward the sickroom door. "Feeding a new calf."

She disappears into the sickroom, and Joseph soon joins me. He is barely down the steps into the parlor pit before we hear Mama's screams. "Help! Help! Help!"

I dash up the stairs toward the sound with Joseph close on my heels. I am horrified and paralyzed by the scene before me. The cow is angrily head-butting Mama against the wall and the steel gate to the pen, over and over and over. Joseph sprints past me with a metal pipe he has grabbed. He lands a well-aimed blow on the cow's skull, driving her backward. I take the opportunity to grab Mama, and pull her from the pen to safety. Blood pours from Mama's head, and she collapses on the floor at my feet. My heart pounds in my chest. I start to feel faint too. I send Joseph off to find Pappy while I try to attend to Mama. Finally, she is able to stand with my help, but her left arm hangs limp. Pappy brings the car around to take her to the emergency room while Joseph and I return to the milking. My hands shake so badly that I can hardly put the milkers on.

Mama is admitted to the hospital from the ER with numerous injuries. There are large bruises on her thighs, lower back, and left arm, as well as a scalp laceration needing seven stitches. She also has a dislocated shoulder and a torn ligament on her left collarbone. The most concerning issue, though, is her heart. It is bruised, and the lab test comes back looking like she has had a heart attack.

I am physically sick about this whole situation. I can't eat, and I can't sleep. *My poor Mama.* And of course, now there is no one to cook for us. I feel like I am about to lose it. *How am I going to handle the household duties too, now, on top of going to school four days per week and taking care of the cows?*

I gather up the breakfast dishes and hurry to wash them before I leave. I want to stop and see Mama at the hospital before I go to class. I am starting to think that things will work out. This is the second day since Mama's accident, and everyone has pitched in to help. Yesterday, friends brought dinner over for us and stayed to do the clothes washing. Last evening, Pappy made supper. Finally, a hired man arrived. Pappy had said yes to an Amish man who came asking for work a few weeks ago. The timing was perfect because the family moved yesterday into the modular home that Pappy had moved onto the farm last December.

Mama is sitting up in bed when I get there. The doctor's report is that her heart enzymes are coming down, allowing for surgery to be planned for tomorrow to repair her shoulder. I chat a little, but I can't stay long. I need to be to literature class by ten o'clock, followed by developmental psychology. I hurry home, then, to clean up and study before milking. Tonight, Grammy and Aunt Harriet are scheduled to arrive by airplane to take over the household duties while Mama is laid up. *Grateful would not be a strong enough word to describe my feelings.*

Spring and summer fly by. The corn and soybeans are all planted by the middle of May. Mama continues to improve from her injuries, and Grammy and Harriet return to Pennsylvania at the end of May. As the summer progresses, I begin to plan for beginning the nursing program in the fall. Nursing 101 and CPR give me ten credits at the college. This will be the biggest academic load I have tried to carry so far. I am glad now that I did not try to take all of the other courses along with nursing. I try to continue working on my sociology course, and I buy an algebra book to refresh my math skills during the summer. In July, I make a shopping trip to buy two uniforms, a sweater, and white shoes. Excitement and anxiety swirl around, all mixed up together inside of me. *I just don't know if I can do this.* The hired man lasted all of two weeks. Then he was gone, so there is no extra help on the farm again.

One Sunday in early August, I decide to try to have a calm, controlled discussion with Pappy. His face is relaxed as I approach him outside the parlor after milking.

"Is there any possibility of hiring someone to milk while I am in school? I am going to be gone up to six hours on some days. If you can't do that, I really wish we could cut back on the number of cows. I just can't keep up with all these cows."

I can see his face muscles tighten.

"I can't make a go of this farm if we don't milk this many cows. This is our livelihood. You knew this when you signed up for the nursing program."

Before I can respond, he turns and walks away. The next evening, Pappy strides into the parlor. A frown creases his forehead, and his eyes bore into me. I look away from the eyes that always seem to pierce my very soul. Without any other preliminaries, he begins.

"How do you think we are going to make it if we have to spend all of our profit on hired help? You have no idea how much money it takes to keep things going on this farm. When I agreed that you could go to school, I expected that you would not let it interfere with your work here. It's time you drop this silly notion and quit school. You can't do your job right here and work as a nurse anyway."

I just stare at him. Then the tears that are always just below the surface begin their cascade down my cheeks. Pappy turns and stomps away. There is no stopping the flood. Tears mingle with the manure and dirt on my hands as I stumble through the rest of the milking chores.

September 5, orientation day for the nursing program, arrives with low-hanging clouds and pattering rain. The atmosphere in our household is just as dark and stormy. I have never before "abandoned" my duties during the fall to take classes. I feel guilty that I am letting my father down and, at the same time, I am determined to build a different life for myself.

The orientation session is from one to four o'clock in the afternoon. During the session, the expectations of the program are laid out for us. My anxiety grows as I listen to the number of nursing-care plans, professional papers, and projects that will be required. I am feeling overwhelmed by the time I hurry to my car for the drive home. *This is never going to work!* The clock is pushing five when I step inside the house and hurry up the stairs to change clothes. The milker pump is sending out its deep throated roar from the barn. At least someone has started the chores. I glance at Pappy's face as I step down into the parlor. His jaw is set, and the facial lines are tight, but he does not say anything as I take his place. I read his body language as disapproval of me, and I feel the familiar churning in my stomach.

At supper, Mama tells us that she has received a phone call informing her that her younger brother has died unexpectedly. She really wants to go to the funeral in Pennsylvania. My breath catches, and I steal a look at Pappy. Her leaving too will leave us very shorthanded at the start of the critical harvest season. What follows are hot angry words between the two of them. I cannot help but feel responsible for this mess. I flee the table.

Hurry! Hurry! Hurry! This is the further stepped-up state of my life. We have four hours of class every afternoon except Tuesday. Then on Friday, because it is our main clinical day, class starts at eight o'clock in the morning. I am sure I smell like the barn most days, as I barely have time to change clothes before I leave home. I have already gotten comments about my dirty fingernails and the need to come to clinical with them clean. I am not sure how one can milk cows twice a day and still have clean fingernails. I do love learning about nursing and interacting with the other students. Just yesterday, we were practicing how to interview patients. It was hilarious. I don't think I have laughed that hard in a long time. Studying is a struggle, though, as every time I sit down, I drift off to sleep. And in between classes and

on my days off, I need to work the care of the cows and calves
into my schedule.

The fall has been rainy. The harvest is behind schedule and
slow. Corn harvest does not even get underway until late October,
making for irritable harvesters. My job, besides taking care of the
cattle, is watching the corn dryer. This is something I can do while
I milk, bed hutches, do bookwork, move cows around, and take
care of new babies. Occasionally, I haul a load of corn, but most
of the fieldwork is left to the menfolk.

November 7 dawns cool but sunny. Today is my first real nursing clinical, but I don't need to leave until noon. I make sure the
corn dryer is started and working properly before returning to the
house to read and study. I check the dryer periodically throughout
the morning. Everything seems to be working well. Then at noon,
I put on my crisp, new, white uniform and drive away to my first
attempt at being a real nurse. I am proud of my new look. It is
six o'clock in the evening again before I am able to slip back into
my barn clothes and start the milking. I try to keep an eye on the
dryer while I milk, but it is time-consuming and tiring to keep
running out of the parlor every half-hour. I am exhausted from
the day and late already with the milking.

Something doesn't sound right as I get on my bike to pedal
out for a delayed dryer check. As I approach, I notice that the
dryer is almost empty. For some reason, the corn load auger did
not start when it should have. This allowed the corn level to slide
below the main drying chamber as it dried without refilling. The
burner has gone out as a result of this. *I do not need this.* I tap the
eye on the fill auger and it restarts, refilling the dryer with wet
corn. After refiring the burner and getting everything back on

track, I return to milking. An hour later, when I check again, the fill auger has failed to stop. A whole load of corn has spilled out over the end of the dryer. *I cannot believe this. I cannot deal with this.* I call for help from Paul.

A few hours later, the combine rolls in from the field and parks. Pappy is not happy with the mess by the dryer, and I am in no mood to be scolded for it. Soon we are engaged in a screaming volley of words over my choice to put my time into nursing school instead of being available full-time to help with the harvest. The next morning, the argument begins again while I am hurrying to get ready for school. *I do not have time for this.* This is the first clinical that I will be providing actual patient care, and I need to be there by eight o'clock. Now I am running late, and my emotions are in turmoil. I cry all the way to school, leaving me in no mood to give patient care. But I force myself to put one foot ahead of the other to get through another day. I am sure my swollen eyes are a dead giveaway to the nursing instructor, as she gently encourages me to share what is wrong. And thus begins a relationship with Patricia, the person who will be my anchor and give me strength in my bid to finally break away from the expectations that bind me.

Several more months pass in this same whirlwind of daily craziness. My only hope is that I will have the strength to make it through the nursing program. In this new year of 1986, I have stopped writing in my diary, as I have done for the past seventeen years. I no longer have the emotional energy to do anything other than what I actually am required to do each day. Pappy, maybe finally realizing that I have no intention of quitting nursing school, hires Tony as a herdsman in late winter. Tony and his wife and children move into the little house by the grain setup. That way, he will be close by and available twenty-four hours a day to work. Tony's responsibilities include helping me with the milking and taking care of some of the other numerous chores. I am thankful for his help, but I soon discover that, even though he is married, I am having the same struggle that I had with the previous herdsman several years earlier. Tony loves to get a rise out of me by pinching my butt as I go by. *Do all men think that women are sex objects to be played with?* Finally I have had it.

"Leave your hands off of me," I snap at him. We fall into an understanding that I won't tolerate his nonsense. Everything goes well for about three months. Then Tony announces that he is quitting.

I turn from the cow that I have been putting the milking machine on and come face to face with Tony. Before I can make any move, he scoops me up in his arms and plants a long firm kiss on my lips.

"That's for playing hard to get." He says. He laughs and then sets me down on the parlor floor. He turns, sprints up the parlor steps, and out of my life. Joseph stands speechless at the other end of the parlor. I am embarrassed, and I am furious. Tony has waited until his last day to take liberties that are not his to take, knowing that he will not face any retribution for his actions.

I do not dare tell Pappy, as he has already made the statement, "Once Tony is gone, I am never hiring another herdsman." In the first place, I don't have a relationship with my father that allows me to tell him such things. And secondly, I do not wish to risk sabotaging any chance that he might hire another man to help by giving him a valid reason to not do so.

I struggle to find some reason to get out of bed each morning. I still have another year of nursing school left. I am angry most of the time. I feel trapped, and thoughts of ending my life begin to enter my mind. Another inner voice reminds me, though, that being dead won't be of much help to me personally.

Alternatively, I begin to formulate my plan of escape. My first step is to order a bunch of ear tags. I want all the cows to have ear tags and all the herd books to be fully up to date so that when the time comes, I will not feel guilty about leaving everything in a mess. I personally know what each cow's number is, even if the tag is missing, but someone else would not. My goal is to, one by one, catch those needing tags as they come through to calve or be bred or need some other kind of treatment. I just don't have time to catch them for this specific purpose all at one time. Methodically and secretly preparing for my final departure gives me the motivation I need to face each day. I just need to make it through one more year.

Chapter 10

FLIGHT TO FREEDOM

I stack three straw bales onto the wheelbarrow in the mid-morning summer sun. Today is my self-imposed scheduled day to bed the calf hutches. The first year of nursing classes has been done for a few weeks now, so I have been spending all my time with the usual activities needed to care for our two-hundred-cow dairy herd. I notice that Pappy is hooking the wagon to the pickup by the house. He and my brothers are going to get a load of straw this morning that he has bought. We are about out of straw, and it will be a few more weeks until oats harvest. As I wheel the straw bales toward the first row of hutches, Pappy walks toward me. His jaw is set, and his brow is scrunched into determined lines.

"You are not bedding hutches today," he informs me.

My anger is instantly triggered. *This is ridiculous.* "And why not?" I demand. "I always bed hutches on Wednesdays."

"I said you are not going to bed hutches today, and that's the way it is going to be," he retorts. With that he turns and walks away. I swear aloud at his retreating back, something that I have never done before. He just keeps walking. I have always made the decision as to when to bed the hutches, so I see this as one more area in which Pappy is trying to exert his control. I am frustrated, and I am at my wits' end with the increasingly tight control of every aspect of our lives. Just a couple of evenings ago, he came into the parlor and ordered Joseph and me to shut the parlor entrance doors between group changes. The day was suffocatingly hot, and having the door open allowed a small breath of cooler air to enter. The only reason he could give was, "that isn't the way I am going to have things done around here."

I watch Pappy's retreating back with a sense of despair. I do not know this man or respect him any longer. I am at the end of my rope. I have no desire to do anything. I just cannot go on. I sit on a straw bale for a while and try to decide what to do. I am sick to my stomach. The black cloud that always threatens to overtake me descends like a shroud around me. *I just want to die.*

I had not planned to leave just yet. I have not finished getting the cow records up to snuff. Now, I no longer care. I walk slowly to the house and up the stairs to my bedroom. Mama is sleeping on the couch. I pull out Mama's old suitcase that is stored in my closet and begin to throw the basic items that I will need into it. Then I sit for minutes at a time on the bed, trying to decide if I can really go through with this. My mind is in turmoil. Every muscle in my body contracts as fear grips me. *If I fail this time, my life is over.* I finally snap the suitcase shut and tiptoe down the stairs to the kitchen. Mama is still asleep on the couch.

"Mama," I say, and her eyes flicker open. "I'm leaving."

Without giving her time to respond, I turn, pick up the suitcase, and hurry toward "my" car. I am well aware that Pappy has never put "my" car into my name. Therefore, I don't know whose car it really is. I waste no time in throwing the suitcase into the backseat and plunking myself behind the wheel. I do not want to allow Mama any time to try to stop me. Having been jerked from her sleep by my sudden announcement, Mama gathers herself up to follow me. I see her standing, bewildered, on the mudroom entry steps as I drive away.

Joseph tells me later that the menfolk returned from getting the straw in time for dinner. They sat down at the table, and dinner was eaten in the same strained silence that was often the case in those days. Mama did not say anything. It wasn't until later in the afternoon that Pappy finally noticed that I was missing.

"Where's Amanda?"

"She packed and left." Mama finally shares the information.

Apparently, the challenge must be met in the only way that they know how: by trying to squelch the rebellion. Mama makes a call to the sheriff's department that afternoon, reporting me as a runaway. They chuckle when they learn that I am twenty-eight years old.

The tears roll down my cheeks as I drive. I do not know what I am going to do, but I steer the car west, toward the home of my nursing instructor. I hope that she is home. I hope that she will give me a place to stay until I can get a job and find a place to live. I know that it is a huge emotional risk for someone to get involved in my messed-up life. But Patricia opens the door to my ringing of her doorbell. She welcomes me with open arms. Soon I am settled into a spare bedroom. Later, we talk about my options. I can possibly get a job at a nursing home as a nursing assistant. As a current nursing student, I have a good chance at that.

I also call a recently married young couple, Darrell and Yolanda Schowalter, from the Moorland Mennonite church. I ask them if I can rent a room from them. I know that I am risking detection by contacting anyone who might have a connection with my parents. I have no intention of calling Mama and Pappy and letting them know where I am. That could only result in being dragged back home again. I am also not sure if anyone from the church will want to stick their neck out to help me, but I need to try. No one has been able to stand up to Pappy during Joseph's or my past attempts at making our own decisions in life. I find out later that my fears are not unfounded, as the minister is the first one who gets a call from Mama. Thankfully, he does not give them any information as to my whereabouts.

The next morning, I dress in the best clothes that I have and drive to the nursing home on the edge of town. I fill out an application and then am told that if I want to wait, they will interview me that day. By noon, I have landed a part-time job at the nursing home. I will be working Friday evening and Saturday and Sunday during the upcoming school year. During this summer, I will be able to pick up other evenings and days if desired. My starting date is the following Monday. I take my good news back to Patricia. Now I have a job and a place to stay.

Patricia encourages me to call my parents, now that I have a plan. "If you were a mother, you would want to know that your child is okay," she says.

I hesitate. My gut tells me that no good can come from calling them. I don't know if I can stand up to my father. But the soft spot in my heart argues that she is right. Parents should not have to worry about what has happened to their offspring.

My hand shakes as I pick up the phone to dial. I hold my breath as it rings.

"Hello."

Pappy's voice.

"This is Amanda. I just wanted you to know that I am fine and doing okay, so that you won't worry."

"Where are you? You need to stop this nonsense right now and come home."

I take a deep breath and make the plunge. "I am not coming

home. I have a job at the nursing home now and a place to live."
I wait for his reply.

"Then you need to quit the job and come home. I am going to
come and find you if you don't come home on your own."

Why did I make this call? "All right," I finally agree, "I will
come home and help when I am not working until school starts
again. I will try to get all the records up to date for you. But I am
not quitting my job. I just got this job, and I am going to keep it."

I am shaking all over by the time I hang up. I collapse in the
chair, exhausted. *What have I done?*

With a stabbing pain in my chest and knots in my stomach,
I drive up the familiar driveway and park in front of the house
the next day.

Pappy is waiting. "Give me the keys to the car," he demands.
With a sigh, I comply.

"Now you are not going anywhere."

*Nothing has changed. So this is how he thinks he is going to control
the situation. And I thought this was my car.* I am infuriated. This
time, I am determined that I am not going to lose.

"You will give me back the keys, or I will have someone come
and get me." I hold out my hand. He sizes me up and finally drops
the keys in my outstretched palm.

Then, he tries a different tactic, "If I pay you for your work,
will you stay?"

I am not interested in staying by this point under any circumstances. "No, I don't want your money. I do think I deserve
something for all the years that I have put in here, but right now,
I just want out."

"I'll try to see that you get something," he murmurs, but no
specifics are decided upon.

A part of me still believes, based on earlier years, that deep
down, under his hard-core controlling behavior, there must be a

part of him that still cares for me as his child. In spite of his words earlier, that if we left the farm, we would get nothing, I do not really believe it. I have seen those words as a tool to manipulate and control, nothing more. Consequently, I still believe that in the end, he will come around to giving me what I deserve for all my years of work on the farm.

I spend the weekend at home doing all the things that I have always done. Then I drive away on Sunday evening to my new life. I load the car with my few remaining possessions. Not only do I start my nursing assistant job on Monday, but I visit the local car dealer. There, I spend $6,000 of my money to buy a 1984 Oldsmobile. I leave the Mercury in the garage at the farm. I have no intention of ever again being controlled by someone withholding my means of transportation.

By the end of the week, I am situated in my room at the Schowalters'. I spend my days off at home milking and taking care of the cows for the rest of the summer, returning to my room and my job on days that I am scheduled at the nursing home.

I crawl out of bed at six thirty in my room at Darrell and Yolanda's. The October sun streams through the window. It seems strange to dress and eat breakfast without hurrying. There are no cows to milk. I have noticed over the last few weeks that my clothes are getting tighter. I am going to have to seriously modify my eating habits. I begin to joke with people who are trying to lose weight that I have the perfect solution for them— just go to work for my parents. I am out the door and off to class by eight thirty. School is back in session, and my days during the week are filled with classes, studying, and clinical. On the weekend, there is work at the nursing home and social

interactions at church. Tonight, I will be going to the home
of Saul Schowalters, the Mennonite bishop, for supper. I have
made a decision that I am going to join the church. None of us
has officially belonged to any Mennonite church since moving
to Minnesota. And none of us has been able to take communion
since Pappy refused to drop his involvement with the pipeline
protest group. I am sick and tired of belonging nowhere, of
being on the outside looking in. Maybe now, I can build a new
reputation for myself and leave behind the stigma that has become attached to my family. Subconsciously, I think my choice
is an additional means of declaring my independence. But I
also realize that my choice will be seen by Pappy and Mama
as a betrayal of them and possibly further drive the wedge into
whatever relationship we have left.

Part of me, as well, is consumed by a sense of guilt that I have
left the rest of my family with more work than they can possibly
do without another person to help. I have always been proud that
I could do just as much as the boys, and I want my father to be
pleased with me. As a result, I decide to keep going home to help
during any break from school, until Pappy is able to hire enough
help. At least, from my perspective, the way to make things work
is to hire more help or, alternatively, cut back. I am sure that,
eventually, Pappy will come to his senses and make the necessary
changes.

The first break from school comes in mid-October, during
MEA week. My twenty-ninth birthday was just two days ago.
I get up at six in the morning and drive home. Mama is cheer-
ful and seems happy to see me. I give her a big hug. I warily
wonder what they are all thinking, but no one says anything.
I mistakenly make the assumption that we have all moved on,
into a level of acceptance. I have always felt bad that helping
Mama in the house was never a priority with Pappy, so I clean

the upstairs for her before heading out to the barn. There, I find the new hired man struggling to find some specific cows. I lend a helping hand. Then, I look over the herd books. There are six calves that need to be photographed and entered into the young stock book. So the afternoon is spent positioning legs and trying to snap the perfect picture of each calf. Before I know it, Mama is lining up pails with milk and water to quench the thirst of the thirty calves in the hutches. I help her lug the heavy pails out, four at a time. The calves dance around, eagerly anticipating their favorite time of day. It is a game to see if we can get a pail inside the wire fence before a bobbing head upends it. Finally, bubbles rise out of the milk as the overeager youngster dives with her nose to the bottom of the pail. Once the calves are fed, I offer my services to help milk. I believe my days at home are like a penance for me. I pay my dues to my family so that I can go back to my new life, having assuaged my guilt for another few weeks.

As I walk across the platform to receive my diploma, I stand tall and proud in my cap and gown. This evening in May 1987 is the graduation ceremony for the associate degree in nursing program. It is my first graduation ever. *I have made it!* And I have a 4.0 grade point average to put on my resume. I am even more thrilled that Mama, Joseph, and Pappy have come to my graduation. I have no idea what to think about Paul. He avoids me most of the time now, but I hope he will eventually get over his hurt at my "abandonment." Mama came earlier, to the pinning ceremony as well. Maybe this is an indication that we are making progress in moving on. Ironically, Mama retired from nursing earlier this year, at age sixty-two, while I am just starting out, symbolically taking her place. I have not been this happy for a long time.

My room is chilly this Monday morning. I can hear the rain-drops on the roof above me as I dress for work. Today is my last day as a nursing assistant at the nursing home. It has provided me with the income to survive financially during my last year of the nursing program. The day is a whirlwind of baths, feeding people, and tucking them in for their afternoon naps. Before I know it, I am back in my room. I finish packing the last of my clothes and belongings and load them into the car. With sadness, I wave goodbye to Darrell and Yolanda. I am forever grateful for their kindness in opening their home and hearts to me. But this chapter of my life is over, and I am leaving to move back home · for the summer. That way, I can help on the farm when I am not working in the city or going to school again. I am looking for-ward to beginning my new job tomorrow at the hospital. I have also decided to pursue my four-year degree. In keeping with my decision, I have signed up for statistics at the state university for the summer session. I spend the evening unpacking and settling back into my old room at the farm.

The summer flies by in a whirlwind of activity. I work nights at the hospital, so I have some time during each day to bed hutches, take calf pictures, update the cow records, and of course, help milk. And then there is the studying to squeeze in.

Today, I came home from work and lay down for a couple of hours of sleep. Empty boxes are scattered all over my bedroom, waiting to be filled. After dinner, I begin packing clothes and anything that I want to take with me. This will be my final move away from home. I have found a one-bedroom, furnished, ground-floor apartment in Superior, close to the hospital. I have fallen in love with it.

The milk pump has been sending out its laborious roar for a couple of hours before I step in to help finish up. Pappy is helping in the parlor, and I smile at him.

"You think you are so much better than the rest of us, don't you?" He throws the barb my way. My happiness is instantly driven away. I retreat into my own world. The anger burns in my chest as I drive to work. *So what!* I tell myself. *I am gone from here in three days, and I really don't care what he thinks.* But inside, I do care, and my anger turns into a depression that hangs over me for a week.

Three months have gone by. I am jolted awake at two thirty in the afternoon, after a night shift, by the ringing of the telephone.

"Hello," I groggily intone into the phone.

"This is Joseph. Will you come and get me? I need to get out of here."

Now I am wide awake. My mind races. I am torn as to how to respond. I have deluded myself into thinking that finally I have achieved some degree of acceptance of my own leaving, and I am not sure I want to stir the quagmire again so soon. *How are Pappy and Mama going to take this?*

"I don't really want to get involved," I tell him.

"Just get me out of here, and give me a ride to the bus station. I can take care of myself from there," he pleads.

I pause while I try to decide what to do. I know how hard it was for me to leave and how everyone was reluctant to help for fear of Pappy. *If I don't help him, no one else is going to. Certainly, Joseph deserves to escape as much as I did.*

"All right," I give in. "I'll come and get you tomorrow afternoon."

I am shaking as I hang up the phone. I know there will be ramifications for helping him. I also have no idea if Pappy and Mama are even aware of his plan to leave. I try to study for the rest of the day, but I can't think straight. I am stunned at this turn of events. My stomach churns, and my heart palpitates from the anxiety.

I try to swallow the lump in my throat as I drive up the driveway and park in front of the house the next afternoon. I am queasy and lightheaded. Joseph comes out of his bedroom, carrying the infamous suitcase. Pappy and Mama sit in the living room, sobbing. The tears start to roll down my cheeks too. I feel sorry for these people who are my parents. They are crying because their children have "abandoned" them. They are heartbroken that their dream of us all farming together has been dashed.

"How are we going to make it now?" is their plaintive question to us.

I do not answer. There is no answer that they can hear.

"Come on. Let's go." I nod at Joseph and jerk my head toward the door. We climb into the car and drive away.

On the drive back to Superior, Joseph tells me about the abuse from Pappy that has continued since I left—of hiding in the corn crib on days when Pappy was mad to stay out of his way—and of finally taking him up on his continual refrain of: "If you don't like how we do things around here, you can just leave."

Joseph stays with me for the next two days, while we purchase a bus ticket for Missouri. Joseph, much like me, has been planning for an escape someday. His plan is to hire on with a Mennonite group of young fellows who make their living by building layer houses for chickens. I worry about him, though. He has never been allowed to use the telephone, to drive a car to town, to have a checking account, to explore the world on his own. He is twenty-nine years old with very few skills and only a correspondence-course high school education.

November 17 dawns cloudy and cold. A mixture of rain and snow drifts from the sky. Joseph drives me to work this morning so I don't have to walk in the wet, sloppy precipitation. Then he goes shopping with my car. As soon as I get home, we snap his only earthly possessions into his suitcase and drive to the home of one of the ministers at the Moorland Mennonite church. The minister there has agreed to take Joseph to a different town to catch the bus for Missouri. I hug Joseph tightly.

"Good-bye brother. Take care of yourself. Call me and let me know how you are doing."

I turn, climb into my car, and drive away. I pray that his life may be blessed in a different environment, as mine has been.

37483349R00140

Made in the USA
Lexington, KY
03 December 2014